RECLAIMING

the WESLEYAN
SOCIAL
WITNESS

OFFERING CHRIST

L. Faye Short
and
Kathryn D. Kiser

RECLAIMING
WESLEYAN
SOCIAL
WITNESS

OFFERING CHRIST

Providence House Publishers
WWW.PROVIDENCEHOUSE.COM
FRANKLIN, TENNESSEE

Printed in the United States of America

12	11	10	09	08	1	2	3	4	5

Library of Congress Control Number: 2007943846

ISBN: 978-1-57736-409-2

Unless otherwise noted, all Scripture quotations are taken from the New King James Version/Thomas Nelson Publishers, Nashville: Thomas Nelson Publishers. Copyright © 1982. Used by permission. All rights reserved.

Scripture quotations marked NIV are taken from HOLY BIBLE, NEW INTER-NATIONAL VERSION®. Copyright © 1973, 1978, 1984 by International Bible Society. Used by permission of Zondervan Publishing House.

Cover design by LeAnna Massingille and Joey McNair
Page design by Joey McNair

PROVIDENCE HOUSE PUBLISHERS
238 Seaboard Lane • Franklin, Tennessee 37067
www.providencehouse.com
800-321-5692

CONTENTS

PREFACE

John Wesley commissioned Thomas Coke as superintendent of American Methodism in September 1784 and sent him to America with the admonition, "Offer them Christ." The first American bishop, Francis Asbury, who was ordained superintendent on December 27, 1784, sent forth hundreds of circuit riders to spread Scriptural holiness across the land. So began the auspicious Methodist societies across America, with roots deep in the soil of the new republic. The message of Methodism, with its emphasis upon personal conversion, inward piety, and outward good works, would permeate the very fabric of the nation. Early circuit riders and camp meetings (often conducted in cooperation with the Presbyterians), created a religious and social structure that provided a solid foundation for democracy and freedom—from East to West, as the frontier expanded. This current *Book of Discipline* statement epitomizes the early Methodist concept that salvation and social witness go hand-in-hand:

> Our struggles for human dignity and social reform have been a response to God's demand for love, mercy, and justice in the light of the Kingdom. We proclaim no *personal gospel* that fails to express itself in relevant social concerns; we proclaim no *social gospel* that does not include the personal transformation of sinners. (*The Book of Discipline of The United Methodist Church 2004*, pg. 49)

Even so, there is a great divide within The United Methodist Church regarding these two essential components. While some churches proclaim the Gospel of Christ for the transformation of sinners—and advocate for a strong social witness within the culture—others divide along the line of neglecting either the Gospel or the social witness.

We have embarked on this book project because we believe it has the potential of making a substantive contribution to the life of The United Methodist Church.

We believe The United Methodist Church needs not only to reclaim a Wesleyan social witness, but even more important, to rediscover the core of the Wesleyan witness—faith working by love. In rediscovering this, we will find the catalyst for a personal and social witness that is as relevant to the twenty-first century as it was to John Wesley's eighteenth century.

In Wesley's sermon "Salvation by Faith," preached at the University of Oxford just eighteen days after his famed heart-warming religious experience at Aldersgate, Wesley asked and answered the question, "What, then, is saving faith?"

"Saving faith is resting upon Christ as our atonement and our life—a savior who gave himself for us and lives in us. The result of saving faith is uniting with Christ, and adhering firmly to him 'who became for us wisdom from God, and righteousness and sanctification and redemption.' In a word, Christ is our salvation."[1]

Wesley made it clear that, " . . . we are speaking of a faith that is the foundation of all good works and of all holiness."[2]

Indeed, faith working by love is the core Methodist value that we must reclaim if we are to obtain personal salvation, live a life of holiness and do good works, and have a truly Wesleyan social witness in the world. Wesley reminds us in his sermon "The Almost Christian," "It is crucial to keep in mind that the kind of faith which fails to produce repentance, love, and good works is not genuine living faith."[3]

Reclaiming the Wesleyan Social Witness: Offering Christ is co-authored by L. Faye Short and Kathryn D. Kiser. Direct contributors to the book include: Mrs. Judi Arnold; Rev. Dr. Chris Bounds, associate professor of Theology at Indiana Wesleyan University; Dr. Janice Shaw Crouse, author, columnist, and director of Cross Communications; Rev. Dr. James V. Heidinger, president of Good News; Dr. H. T. Maclin, former General Board of Global Ministries missionary and president emeritus of The Mission Society; Rev. Dr. Jim Thobaben, professor of Church in Society at Asbury Seminary; Rev. Dr. Tom Thomas; and Rev. Dr.

Kenny Yi. We are deeply indebted to these women and men for their contributions to this project.

Without the contributions of the individuals listed above, this book would not have been written. You will find their contributions intermingled within the text of the book. Where approval was granted, the papers submitted for use in this book are available in their entirety.

In his sermons and writings, John Wesley often posed questions, which he then answered. Each chapter of this book begins with a question posed by an imagined layperson in the pew answered by John Wesley through his writings. The need for the Wesleyan message could not be greater than it is in the twenty-first century.

RECLAIMING

the WESLEYAN SOCIAL WITNESS

OFFERING CHRIST

Chapter One
The Historical Wesleyan Witness

Person in the Pew (Pip): The Methodist movement became the recipient of the spiritual heritage of both you and your brother, Charles. What do you value most from your family history, and how did your home life shape who you became?

Wesley: Charles and I, along with our other brothers and sisters, were raised as faithful adherents to the teachings of the Church of England. Even so, we were not far removed from the dissenters. Our great-grandfather, Bartholomew, and grandfather, John Wesley, chose the path of Nonconformity in 1662—as did our mother's father, Samuel Annesley. However, our parents, Samuel and Susanna, returned to the Church of England.

    The Bible, *The Book of Common Prayer*, and the Homilies[1] were central to our upbringing—our mother used them to teach us at home prior to our entry into the university. Later in my life these were still foundational. I wrote in 1760, "I do not defend or espouse any other principles, to the best of my knowledge, than those which are plainly contained in the Bible as well as in the Homilies and *The Book of Common Prayer*."[2]

Pip: When I think about your family heritage and your accomplishments, I wonder why you were still seeking something beyond what you had found. How long after your ordination did you feel and know all was well with your soul?

Wesley: Ah, it was ten long years! Before my conversion experience, I struggled to find acceptance with God. I wrote to a friend, "All my works, my righteousness, my prayers, need an atonement for themselves. . . . God is holy, I am unholy. . . . Yet I hear a voice (and is it not the voice of God?) saying, 'Believe, and thou shalt be saved.'"[3]

Charles found rest to his soul on the twenty-first of May, 1738, and shared, "I now found myself at peace with God, and rejoiced in hope of loving Christ."[4] Three days later, after much personal struggle, I stood on the same sure ground with Charles and later wrote, "I felt my heart strangely warmed. I felt I did trust Christ, Christ alone for salvation; and an assurance was given to me that He had taken away my sins, even mine, and saved me from the law of sin and death."[5]

Together Charles and I sang the words he had penned:

> Where shall my wondering soul begin?
> How shall I all to heaven aspire?
> A slave redeemed from death and sin,
> A brand plucked from eternal fire,
> How shall I equal triumphs raise,
> Or sing my great Deliverer's praise?[6]

What a glorious day! Thank you for reminding me of it. God be praised.

LAYING THE FOUNDATION

A Family Legacy

Samuel Wesley and Susanna Annesley Wesley chose to be faithful members of the Church of England. By contrast, Samuel's grandfather and father, and Susanna's father, had been among the Dissenters who refused to sign the Act of Uniformity in 1662. Samuel served as the rector of Epworth Church in Lincolnshire. The couple had nineteen children—John was the fifteenth and Charles the eighteenth.

The Wesleys's upright English ancestors passed to them a living legacy of their love of the Bible and their adherence to Church of England tradition. This was expressed in *The Book of Common Prayer*, homilies, and doctrinal articles and creeds. The way of life at Epworth had a lasting influence upon the lives of John and Charles Wesley.

Indeed, reverence of Scripture had family history. One grandfather, Samuel Annesley, became the leader of the London Dissenters and a noted expositor of the Bible. Samuel Wesley wrote *Life of Christ, The History of the Old and New Testament in Verse*, and was completing a Latin work on Job at the time of his death.

One sees this influence in John and Charles; reading their writings is like reading the Biblical text. It is clear these men were well-acquainted with the Bible and its teachings. John wrote in the preface to his standard sermons:

> I want to know one thing—the way to heaven. I want to know how to land safely on that happy shore. . . . God himself has descended to teach the way; it is for this very purpose that Christ came from heaven. He has written the way in a book. O, give me that book! At any price give me the Book of God! I have it, and it contains knowledge enough for me![7]

The Church of England tradition was also cherished by the Wesley family. Susanna wrote manuals of biblical instruction and an exposition of the Apostles' Creed for her children.[8] Moreover, *The Book of Common Prayer* had a major role in shaping the spiritual understanding of the Wesley children. It served as a companion to the Bible, grounding them in the doctrine and history of the Church, as well as the teaching of the reformers.

Home schooling and religious instruction were provided from a very early age. "Our children were taught, as soon as they could speak, the Lord's Prayer, which they were made to say at rising and bedtime constantly; to which, as they got bigger, were added a short prayer for their parents, and some collects, a short catechism, and some portion of Scripture, as their memories could bear," Susanna wrote.[9] It is noteworthy that the sons went on to win high distinction at famous public schools Westminster, Charterhouse, and Oxford.

This legacy of faith would propel John and Charles toward religious study and practice—and toward a heart-hunger for favor with God that would ultimately lead them to saving faith.

Outside Influences

In 1725, John reported, "When I was about twenty-two, my father pressed me to enter into holy orders." This path led John to spiritual discoveries in the literature of Christian writers, including Bishop Jeremy Taylor and William Law from the Church of England; and Thomas á Kempis from the Catholic past.[10] The writings of these men and others challenged and shaped the thinking of John and, no doubt, Charles Wesley.

In early 1729, a number of influences converged in John's life which convinced him "not only to read, but to study the Bible, as the one, the only standard of truth, and the only model of pure religion." At this time Wesley established clearly in his mind the *telos* (completion or end) of Christianity—holiness of heart and life, holiness capable of changing the world. The question of how holiness of heart and life comes about in an individual and in the world, however, eluded Wesley at this early stage in his theological understanding.[11]

Another providential intervention leading the two Wesley brothers toward the spiritual peace they desired took place on their journey to America.

> The Wesley brothers went to Georgia as ordained clergymen of the Church of England. John was ordained priest in 1728, Charles a few days before embarking for America.
>
> In October 1735, the brothers sailed for the colony of Georgia, Charles to serve as Secretary to Oglethorpe the Governor, John to be a missionary to the Indians and to act as minister to the Anglican Church in Savannah. . . . It was on this voyage that they were drawn into fellowship with a group of Moravian refugees whose piety and sincerity were to point for them the way to saving faith.
>
> It was Peter Bohler, the Moravian, who brought the Wesleys to the verge of the great discovery.[12]

This initial contact forged a link to the Moravian faith that traced itself back to the heroic John Huss, burned at the stake in 1415, and to the writings of John Wycliffe, which shaped the teaching of Huss.

Back in England, in February 1738, John had a providential meeting with Peter Bohler, Schulius Richter, and Wensel Neisser, who had just arrived from Germany. He helped them secure a place to stay and spent much time in their company. What John saw in the lives of these Moravians caused him to doubt his own worthiness to preach the Gospel. Bohler encouraged John not to give up his calling, but instead to, "Preach faith *till* you have it; and then, *because* you have it, you *will* preach faith."[13]

Ultimately, it was the voice of the great reformer Martin Luther that reached across two centuries and spoke first to Charles, then to John, enabling them both to find the faith they would preach for the remainder of their lives in word, song, and deed.

Receiving the Inheritance

In May 1738, both John and Charles were wrestling within and without for an assurance of their salvation. The prevenient grace (the grace that goes before conversion) that John would identify by name in later teaching was pressing upon them.

Charles was not only distressed of mind, but sick in body. He was lodging in London at the home of a friend, John Bray. Bray's home was a place where seekers like Charles came to pray, converse, and read religious literature. It was here that Charles encountered Martin Luther's *Commentary on the Epistle to the Galatians*. He read:

Who is this "me"? Even I, wretched and damnable sinner, so dearly beloved of the Son of God, that he gave himself for me. If I, then, through works or merits could have loved the Son of God, and so come unto him, what needed he to deliver himself for me? . . .

But because there was no other price either in heaven or on earth, but Christ the Son of God, therefore it was most necessary that he should be delivered for me. Moreover, this he did of inestimable love: for Paul saith, "which loved me." . . .

Read therefore with great vehemency these words, "me" and "for me," and so inwardly practice with thyself, that thou, with a sure faith, mayst conceive and print this "me" in thy heart, and apply it unto thyself, not doubting but thou art the number of those to whom this "me" belongeth.[14]

On Whitsunday, May 21, Charles received the assurance of salvation and was physically healed at the same time. He rejoiced, "I now found myself at peace with God, and rejoiced in hope of loving Christ."

When John heard of Charles's experience, he wrote: "I received the surprising news that my brother had found rest to his soul. His bodily strength returned also from that hour. 'Who is so great a God as our God?'" But for himself, in a letter to a friend written at the same time, he could but say: "All my works, my righteousness, my prayers, need an atonement for themselves. So that my mouth is stopped. I have nothing to plead. God is holy, I am unholy. . . . Yet, I hear a voice (and is it not the voice of God?) saying, 'Believe, and thou shalt be saved.'"[15]

On Wednesday, May 24, 1738, John began his day with the reading of Scripture in the early morning hours. He read 2 Pet. 1:4, "There are given unto us exceeding great and precious promises, even that ye should be partakers of the divine nature." In the afternoon he attended St. Paul's and found in the anthem the same message of promise as he had found in the morning's Scripture. That evening, John's experience culminated at a meeting on Aldersgate Street. John wrote these words, familiar to many, in his journal:

> In the evening I went very unwillingly to a society in Aldersgate Street, where one was reading Luther's preface to the Epistle to the Romans. About a quarter before nine, while he was describing the change which God works in the heart through faith in Christ, I felt my heart strangely warmed. I felt I did trust in Christ, Christ alone for salvation; and an assurance was given me that He had taken away "my" sins, even "mine," and saved "me" from the law of sin and death.[16]

Charles Wesley recounted the end to this memorable day: "Toward ten, my brother was brought in triumph by a troop of our friends, and declared, 'I believe.' We sang the hymn with great joy, and parted with prayer."

Passing On the Inheritance

Prior to their personal, life-changing conversions, John and Charles Wesley had endeavored to live holy lives, to do good works, and to enlist others to join them. The Holy Club at Oxford was established by Charles and later led by John prior to their salvation-by-faith experience. The derisive name "Methodist" was first applied to Charles and his Oxford friends, indicating the studious and devotional rule of life which they followed. Their goals were to converse with young students, visit the prisons, instruct some poor families, and take care of a school and a parish workhouse.[17] After their personal encounters with Christ, the Gospel and social witness of the Wesleys took on a new dimension. With that experience came the understanding that holiness cannot be realized apart from saving faith.

Upon reviewing this historic panorama of Wesley's Christian faith, one could easily visualize the plan of God to preserve the Apostolic faith throughout all generations—nor is it difficult to see the role of Methodism in that process. We are the glad recipients of this heritage.

BUILDING ON THE FOUNDATION

In his paper "The Histoical Wesleyan Witness," Dr. Tom Thomas differentiates between the "personal" and "social" aspects of the Wesleyan witness of Methodism in England and America. *The Book of Discipline* demonstrates the balance that exists between the two when it states that we "proclaim no *personal gospel* that fails to express itself in relevant social concerns; we proclaim no *social gospel* that does not include the personal transformation of sinners."

The Gospel Is Personal

"Personal" is what pertains to, or concerns, the individual. John Wesley's theology is foundationally personal in theology and

> With that experience came the understanding that holiness cannot be realized apart from saving faith.

experience. To ignore or marginalize the personal aspect of theology, in favor of emphasizing the corporate or social, is to eviscerate it and miss it entirely. Although the Scriptures speak to corporate matters, the primary emphasis is individual and personal: each person is individually a sinner and accountable to God, each person is individually loved and chosen, and each person must respond to God's grace on an individual basis. The Gospel is personal, also, in that it is revealed by a personal Savior, reveals a personal God, and demands a personal encounter between the individual penitent sinner and a gracious, forgiving God. The Gospel is personal, finally, in that the beginning of a saving and redeeming knowledge of Jesus Christ is in the individual's heart and soul—the very center of personhood. This experience culminates in the inner, supra-sensory understanding that Christ loved me, and gave Himself for *me*.

The Gospel Is Social

The Gospel is also "social" in several different ways. John Wesley used the term "social holiness" in the preface to his list of poetical works and states "the gospel of Christ knows of no religion, but social; no holiness but social holiness." Wesley was using the term solely to counter a monastic withdrawal away from society. He, thus, insists that a person cannot be personally transformed into the image of Christ and experience sanctification apart from the Christian community. For John Wesley, justification is personal and sanctification is both personal and social. Wesley stated uncompromisingly that social sanctification, which consists only of outward ceremonies and forms—and the doing of much good—is a counterfeit outward religion.

Personal and social holiness work together in a synergistic and cooperative relationship. They act together to increase the effect of one another. Personal growth in holiness combines with outward good works increasing love and good works. Increased zeal and performance of outward good works increases one's zeal for personal experience of inner growth in grace and holiness.

The Personal and Social in Balance

John Wesley and the Methodists are exemplary in Christian history as authentic proponents of both evangelical faith and social love, justification by faith and good works, inward and outward religion, the "personal" and the "social." Through their own personal experience of the love of God and the love of humankind in justification and sanctification, they offered to any who were receptive the possibility of full redemption from ills of soul and body. Holding together both personal pardon and social love, the higher goal of the salvation of souls was the deepest motivation for social mercies of bodies.[18] (Thomas' unpublished essay, "The Historical Wesleyan Witness," is provided in the appendix for further study.)

GRAND SCRIPTURAL DOCTRINES FOR TODAY

Achieving the Balance

> For by grace you have been saved, through faith—
> and not of yourselves, it is the gift of God—
> not by works, lest anyone should boast.
> For we are His workmanship,
> created in Christ Jesus for good works,
> which God prepared in advance that we should walk in them.
> —Eph. 2:8–10

For centuries, tension has existed between salvation by faith alone and our calling to do good works. Most often, we find ourselves on one side or the other while the beautiful balance in Ephesians 2 eludes us. In John Wesley's writings we see the wedding of these two themes in what Albert Outler calls the fusion and balance of God's sovereign grace and man's moral responsibility. Richard Heitzenrater calls it "divine/human cooperation (synergism)." The deep experience of faith obtained when one passes through the threshold of salvation naturally releases a flow of good works. It is through the experience of personal faith we begin to work out our salvation with fear and trembling (Phil. 2:12 NIV).

We see this balance in Wesley's grand scriptural doctrine of salvation, which joined justification and sanctification. Justification is present pardon and acceptance with God through faith in Jesus Christ's atoning death. Sanctification is the radical transformation of the heart, from love of the world to love of God and others. Wesley believed in justification by faith alone; he also believed in the importance of faith being worked out and evidenced in the heart of the believer, first through loving God and then through loving one's neighbor. Sanctification for Wesley was far from works-righteousness. Neither was it characterized by a piety which neglected outward love for others and resulted in withdrawal from the issues that face society.

Wesley distinguished between works of piety (activity aimed at God) and works of mercy (activity aimed at the soul and body of individuals). One was not to be sacrificed at the expense of the other. Even within works of mercy, meeting the physical and material needs of humanity was joined to ministering to spiritual needs. In all his social work, Wesley kept before him a commitment to the higher goal of the salvation of souls. We see this in the way he confronted slavery. While in the American colonies, he preached salvation to the slaves. At the same time, he condemned the institution of slavery and worked for its abolition. The same can be said of his work on behalf of prisoners. His desire for prison reform did not replace his love for prisoners and his desire for their salvation. This balance needs to be recovered today.

Encompassing Rich and Poor

Wesley had a deep love for both the rich and the poor. Though Wesley believed himself an ambassador to the humble, he reached out to all regardless of their social, economic, or educational standing, preaching God's love for all persons.

The concern Wesley showed for the rich moved him to confront materialism as well as hardness of heart. The rich were challenged to do more than just give—Wesley wanted them to understand what life was really like for the poor and to develop true compassion. He also believed they should be educated on these issues so that their alms would not be misused.[19]

> All therefore who desire to escape everlasting fire and to inherit the everlasting kingdom are equally concerned . . . to practice this important duty. It is equally incumbent on young and old, rich and poor, men and women, according to their ability. None are so young, if they desire to save their own souls, as to be excused from assisting their neighbours. None are so poor (unless they want the necessaries of life) but they are called to do something . . . for the relief and comfort of their afflicted.[20]

Wesley called everyone to the cardinal point of ethics that is to be applied to the whole of Christian life: "Loving God with all our heart, soul, and strength, as having first loved us, as the fountain of all the good that we have received, and of all we ever hope to enjoy; and loving every soul which God hath made, every man on earth, as our own soul."[21]

Wesleyan Cultural Influence

During Wesley's lifetime, many people who had been poor found their lives changed for the better as they turned to God and appropriated holy living. As people began to value themselves as God values them, they dealt with sins such as sloth, drunkenness, and self-indulgence, and were encouraged to develop virtues of thrift, industry, honesty, sobriety, and generosity.[22] Along with the development of capitalism, this allowed many in the Methodist movement to improve their lot in life. This is particularly interesting because, unlike today, class structure in the eighteenth century made social mobility very difficult. Nevertheless, men raised their standard of living when they grew in holiness and followed Wesley's teaching on the use of money—"gain all you can, save all you can, and give all you can." Wesley believed this principle would both provide for those in want and protect the giver from the deceitfulness of riches.

Wesley's admonitions on the use of money and proper attitudes toward the poor make it clear that his concerns for humankind ran deeper than the alleviation of economic want or social mobility. Richard Heitzenrater summarizes Wesley's view on money:

> [Wesley's] basic goal in this regard was for Methodists to imitate the life of Christ, not improve the national economy. He conceived of the problem theologically in terms of love of God and love of neighbor rather than in terms of defining minimum wage, improving the country's wealth or solving a social problem.[23]

When Alexis de Tocqueville traveled to England in the 1830s, he observed that the English nobility were fully engaged in the reconstitution of religious and moral living that was taking over the country which would not have been seen a half century earlier.[24] Herbert Schlossberg remarks that the number of societies that sprang up has never been accurately catalogued; one Bible society alone had over one hundred thousand members.

> They banded together in huge numbers to form societies for helping the poor, evangelizing among an amazingly diverse array of groups, reforming morals, suppressing vice, improving the lot of prisoners, rescuing prostitutes from their economic distress and therefore their bondage, distributing religious literature and promoting foreign missions.[25]

Averting a Revolution

There has been much speculation about the role the Methodist movement had on the social transformation of England. De Tocqueville believed England had experienced a bloodless revolution in the most positive sense. The spiritual revival begun by the Wesleys and other religious leaders such as George Whitfield is viewed by some historians as a major factor in averting a revolution. Moral and ethical transformation, coupled with social advocacy, created a measure of upward mobility for the lower class and compelled the English aristocracy to address the social inequalities of the day. Other historians see the revival playing a negative role by preventing revolution, which they believe would have brought about more extensive social reforms. The fact remains that England, unlike its neighbor France, did not experience a bloody conflict.

Retaining the Wesleyan Social Witness

To avert a costly revolution in terms of lost human life is remarkable. Equally remarkable was the work of William Wilberforce and his colleagues. Their social advocacy sprung from a deep personal Christian commitment to love God and neighbor and resulted in the eventual abolition of the slave trade in England. Wesley encouraged Wilberforce in his campaign to rid England of slavery.

Nevertheless, over the centuries, John Wesley's concept of social witness has been taken in directions he would have counseled against. We must use caution today when the social witness of Wesley is used to justify any number of social measures that are before the church. All social remedies do not correspond with a Christian worldview or with a Wesleyan point of view. Herbert Schlossberg reminds us that our time is not so different from the eighteenth century and our challenge just as promising:

> The lamentations about contemporary American society—indeed of Western societies in general—seem little different from those heard in the eighteenth century and the early years of the nineteenth. The empty religiosity coexisting with open contempt for the Christian heritage of the nation, the widespread hypocrisy, the general lawlessness, and the political corruption were similar.

All social remedies do not correspond with a Christian worldview or with a Wesleyan point of view.

Change the time-specific terminology and examples in William Wilberforce's *Practical View of the Prevailing Religious System of Professed Christians* (1797) and you might think it was written two centuries later.

Yet there seemed to be remarkably little hand-wringing in Wilberforce and his merry band of anti-slavers. Full of hope, they did their duty to God and men as they were given light, braved the setbacks, and did not seem amazed at their great successes. It was as if they believed that God was ultimately in charge and they had only to be faithful to their charges. There is no reason that that experience could not be repeated today, despite the widespread pessimism. After all, it was only two years from the time Bishop Butler announced to the world that Great Britain had decided that Christianity was fictitious that John Wesley found spiritual life in Christ and the renewal of the entire society began its course.[26]

Chapter Two
The Priority of the Gospel

Pip: Tension exists in our day between those who hold to a gospel of social holiness and those who hold to a gospel of personal holiness. What is your position on these two understandings of the Gospel?

Wesley: I find your question confusing, for there is only one Gospel, and it leads to saving faith. Saving faith is resting upon Christ as our atonement and our life—a savior who gave himself for us and lives in us. The result of saving faith is uniting with Christ, and adhering firmly to him "who became for us wisdom from God, and righteousness and sanctification and redemption." In a word, Christ is our salvation.[1] I would trust it is understood that . . . we are speaking of a faith that is the foundation of all good works and of all holiness.[2] It is crucial to keep in mind that the kind of faith which fails to produce repentance, love, and good works is not genuine living faith.[3]

Pip: So, you would not separate these two and would hold salvation by faith as the foundation for our personal redemption and as the catalyst for our good works. There would not be a social holiness, but rather a social witness springing from lives changed by the Gospel of Jesus Christ.

Wesley: You understand me correctly. I only recall once in my writings where I used the designation "social holiness," and it had no relation to a social gospel. This was in the preface to my list of poetical works where I wrote that the gospel of Christ knows of no religion, but social, no holiness but social holiness.[4] In this case, I was countering the Christian mystics' notion of holiness that withdraws itself from society into entire seclusion from others. I felt this monastic view tried to build on the foundation of justification by retreating "to the desert" in order to purify the soul. This I roundly denounced.[5] I was affirming my belief that the Christian faith is lived out in community. In speaking of holiness as "social holiness," I was arguing that persons grow in holiness and into the measure of the stature of the fullness of Christ in mutually edifying social company and fellowship.[6]

THE WITNESS OF THE CHURCH

A Foundation for Social Witness

"The Bible calls for personal holiness and for sweeping societal changes; it refuses to substitute private religion for social responsibility or social engagement for personal commitment to God."[7] This statement by Carl F. H. Henry mirrors the thinking of John Wesley.

Bringing the transforming power of the Gospel to bear on all of society is an essential part of the Church's mission. From early Christendom, the church has been a major force in the shaping of culture and government. In our highly partisan and politically charged environment, many find it difficult to articulate general Christian principles when it comes to the church's responsibility in the areas of proclaiming the Gospel and bearing social witness. Yet, the United Methodist *Book of Discipline*'s statement on the proclamation of both a *personal gospel* and a *social gospel* captures it well.

Read a practical application of these principles:

Methodist Sarah Peters was titled by John Wesley a "lover of souls." By self-confession Sarah said she could "not rest day or night, any longer than I am gathering in souls to God." Gifted to seek and save the lost, she was also a constant visitor to London's Newgate prison. She tirelessly cared for and ministered to prisoners. Skimping on her meals and petitioning government officials for pardon on prisoners' behalf, she fell victim to a jailhouse fever and died. Sarah Peters exemplifies the Gospel the Methodists proclaimed. It was a Gospel synchronizing the profoundly "personal" and the ardently "social."[8]

Bringing the transforming power of the Gospel to bear on all of society is an essential part of the Church's mission.

Bearing Social Witness

The social witness of the church is shaped by certain principles. It is important to know those principles and to discern how such principles are reflected in the social witness of the Church. William Temple, a former archbishop of Canterbury and pioneer of the ecumenical movement, believed there were two basic methods that guide the Church's social witness.

> First, the Church must announce Christian principles and point out where the existing social order is in conflict with them. Second, it must then pass on to the Christian citizens, acting in their civic capacities, the task of reshaping the existing order in closer conformity to the principles.[9]

On most issues, we must be careful not to enlist the church in partisan political positions. Why? Because sincere Christians will differ on the political means to good and wholesome ends. And when the church takes a political stand, it can alienate those who view the issue from a different political understanding. In eighteenth century England, William Wilberforce, acting as a Christian citizen and political statesman, carried on his crusade against slavery. That took place in the political arena. The Church's proper role was to support the endeavor by emphasizing Christian principles that citizens could use to evaluate this issue. Enlisting the church in partisan political issues is using the church for a political agenda.

Many Scriptures in the Old and New Testament make it clear that acting justly is part of the Judeo-Christian understanding. While the Church has struggled to balance personal salvation and social witness, there is a basis for our involvement in social and political issues.

> We engage in public life because God created our first parents in his image and gave them dominion over the earth (Gen. 1:27–28). . . . Just governance is part of our calling in creation.
>
> We also engage in public life because Jesus is Lord over every area of life. Through him all things were created (Col. 1:16–17), and by him all things will be brought to fullness (Rom. 8:19–21). To restrict our stewardship to the private sphere would be to deny an important part of his dominion and to functionally abandon it to the Evil One. . . .
>
> When Christians do justice, it speaks loudly about God. And it can show those who are not believers how the Christian vision can contribute to the common good and help alleviate the ills of society.[10]

While the Church has struggled to balance personal salvation and social witness, there is a basis for our involvement in social and political issues.

Christians are involved in social and political issues for a number of reasons. We have genuine concern for the poor and oppressed. We understand that Jesus is Lord over all areas of life. Therefore, Christian witness is appropriate in all segments of life. Christians understand the struggle between good and evil, between God and Satan, for the souls and lives of humanity. We have hope because we believe God, through Christ and through the work of the Holy Spirit, can and will make a difference in the lives of men and women, boys and girls. Although we as Christians are citizens of heaven, we are also citizens of this earth, called to be good neighbors and to work for justice on behalf of our neighbors.

Both liberals and conservatives within the Church claim Jesus' example as their model for preaching the Gospel and doing works of mercy. Yet, many acts of compassion and social witness have become highly politicized, often from a partisan perspective.

> Christians must endeavor consistently to submit our political [social] activity to the lordship of Christ and the authority of the Bible. If our political [social] engagement merely reflects secular political agendas of left or right or even center, our efforts will be largely irrelevant. Only if we allow a biblical worldview and a biblically balanced agenda to guide our concrete political work can we significantly improve the political order.[11]

As we continue in obedience to Christ's command to go into all the world and make disciples, we walk in the footsteps of the apostles, the early church fathers, John Wesley, and countless others through whom the Kingdom broke into human existence.

PROCLAIMING THE GOSPEL

There are clear indicators that United Methodism has boards, agencies, bishops, clergy, and lay members who sincerely believe the Kingdom of God can be advanced almost solely by social means. Their emphasis is on social justice, social gospel, and social actions. Dr. Chris Bounds reminds us of the central position of the preaching of the Gospel as the principal methodology in the witness of the church in the world. "The visible Church of Christ is a congregation of faithful men [and women] in which the pure Word of God is preached" is a foundational statement of the Articles of Religion. The primacy of the proclamation of the Word of God should then be a primary focus of our mission to the world. Where the message of Jesus is preached, where the Word of God is proclaimed, the Kingdom in its life-transforming reign becomes possible. God's reign is not established except through the Christian proclamation of Jesus.

Proclaiming the "pure word of God" has the power of transformation because it is one of the primary means or channels of God's grace in the world. The New Testament makes clear that divine grace is communicated first and foremost through the preaching of the Word of God. This proclamation must center on the life, death, resurrection, and exaltation of Jesus Christ. The United Methodist Church's social witness must be marked by an unapologetic and vocal witness to the Lordship of Jesus Christ. Proclamation without that focus on Jesus Christ has been proven powerless to bring about true, life-transforming change in human lives.

Combining Proclamation and Social Witness

It is critically important for the Church to fulfill its primary role to proclaim and teach the Gospel as revealed in Scripture. Apart from the Gospel, there is no grace made available that can bring about true social change in the world. It is not by accident that it has been in the Christian West that social justice in the world has been most nearly experienced—the abolition of slavery, women's rights, prison reform, concern for the indigent. This has characterized our Western culture in a way that has not characterized any other culture. There is a reason for this—the proclamation of the Gospel in Western culture. In our churches where the Gospel is preached, we train the laity. They are equipped with a solid basis in the Christian worldview and a solid Biblical foundation for evaluating and making judgments. They can then go into the world—into every profession and every institution—not leaving their faith at the door of the church, but taking its truth claims out into the world.

But first, we must be clear about those truth claims. We must have a clear understanding of our mission. If the guiding principles of Christianity are true, then they are universally true. They bring the same benefits to all. The Gospel of Jesus Christ is meant for every nation, every culture, indeed, for the entire world.

To withhold the Gospel from the world is to deny the world the only grace capable of bringing about true and lasting change and transformation. Bounds makes a strong point of this:

> Proclamation of the "pure word of God" has this power because it is one of the primary means or channels of God's grace in the world. In any discussion of God's grace, which may be defined simply as the "unmerited" work of God for humanity, in humanity, and through humanity, the question must be asked, "How does God communicate His grace to people? How does God work in people?" The Scriptures reveal that God communicates His grace through appointed "channels" or "means." While recognizing other means of grace, other channels through which God works, the New Testament makes clear that divine grace is communicated first and foremost through the preaching of the Word of God.[12]

The church will be forever challenged in its missionary efforts to make the Gospel relevant to all cultures. Many factors must be considered in order to bring the Gospel not only to the people in our pews, but also to the people of the world. The social witness of the church is a critical tool in its mission. The missionary work of the church must take into account certain social realities. Yet, the church must strive to ensure that the mission goal from *The Book of Discipline* remains central:

> The mission of the Church is to make disciples of Jesus Christ.
> —Par. 120, *The Book of Discipline*

The church has interpreted this statement in many ways. These interpretations create competing visions of what the mission should look like. For those holding a more liberal perspective, deep concern for societal problems and social justice takes first priority. Many social justice advocates focus less on the personal dimensions of the Gospel. Often the greater evil is viewed as systemic rather than personal. Those holding this view believe that social problems and inequalities should be taken more seriously by those who are theologically conservative within the church. On the other hand, conservative evangelicals are often concerned that the mission of the church has become too focused on humanitarian concerns to the neglect of fulfilling the Church's primary mandate to make disciples of Jesus Christ.

Defining sides is not comfortable, and there are crossovers on the part of sincere Christians. Nevertheless, we should ask if any of us have taken the mission of the church seriously enough. What would our world look like if we were all faithful disciples of Jesus Christ? Author Dallas Willard believes that both liberals and conservatives must come to terms with the implications of making—and being— disciples of Jesus Christ.

> The current position of the church in our world may be better explained by what liberals and conservatives have shared than by how they differ. For different reasons, and with different emphases, they have agreed that discipleship to Christ is optional to membership in the Christian church. Thus, the very type of life that could change the course of human society—and upon occasion has done so—is excluded or at least omitted from the essential message of the church.[13]

This message has implications for all United Methodists who declare their mission to be the making of disciples for Jesus Christ. It poses questions, not just for our boards and agencies, but also for the church at large. Even more important, these are questions for each individual. Are we truly disciples of Jesus Christ? Is He our Savior, our teacher, our guide? Do we concur with John Wesley that the result of saving faith is uniting with Christ, and adhering firmly to Him? As United Methodists, do we see Christ as the one who holds the answers to the human dilemma, both personal and societal?

Willard reminds us:

Nothing less than life in the steps of Christ is adequate to the human soul or the needs of our world. Any other offer fails to do justice to the drama of human redemption, deprives the hearer of life's greatest opportunity, and abandons this present life to the evil powers of the age.[14]

To this we can give a hearty *amen.*

The United Methodist Church's social witness must be marked by an unapologetic and vocal witness to the Lordship of Jesus Christ.

A NEW TESTAMENT REVIEW

Jesus did not attempt to construct a this-world political structure or state. He never intended His kingdom to be identified with an external, outward political organization. He refused to be enthroned as a national, political messiah such as King David. After feeding the thousands in the rural, Galilean countryside, when the crowds sought to make Him king, He hid. When Pilate asked Him if He were the King of the Jews, He replied, "My kingdom is not from this world. If my kingdom were from this world, my followers would be fighting to keep me from being handed over to the Jews" (John 18:36).

Rather, Jesus reveals Himself to be the long-awaited, coming Son of God, the Messiah in whom the Kingdom of God has arrived. He invites all persons to repent and believe in Him for the forgiveness of their sins and to be His disciples in a new, covenant community under His rule. Though He and His disciples are sent into the world, He states the Kingdom of God is not of this world. It transcends this world. In speaking of His disciples and Himself,

He says, "They are not from the world as I am not from the world" (John 17:14).

Therefore, though Jesus' kingdom is not identified with a particular political manifestation of this world but is beyond it, it does remain within particular cultures in this world. It has been said that Christians have one foot on earth and one foot already in heaven! Many Christians realize they live in a fallen culture and world and are subject to "Caesar." This dark world can, however, be influenced and transformed through them who are salt and light.[15]

Christians throughout history have found themselves living in every conceivable political system. Sometimes culture has disliked but tolerated them; other times it has been openly and violently hostile. Sometimes political powers have worked in close cooperation with Christians, but other times lived in tension. Occasionally, Christians have identified culture with Christ. Christians have withdrawn from and also transformed culture. In various situations, Christians have learned to be faithful, obedient, and fruitful.

Jesus and Politics

Certainly the work of Christ is not limited to the salvation and renewal of the individual's soul. It impacts all of life, including the social and political dimension. The work of Christ and His teachings have much to say about how we order our lives both personally and corporately. Still, it is important to remember that Christ dismissed political activity or involvement, particularly when it represented a turning away from His sacrifice on the cross. This is vividly seen in the exchange between Jesus and Satan during the temptation of Jesus found in Matthew 4:1–11:

> Again the devil took him to a very high mountain and showed him all the kingdoms of the world and their splendor. "All this I will give you," he said, "if you will bow down and worship me." Jesus said to him, "Away from me, Satan! For it is written: 'Worship the Lord your God, and serve him only'" (v. 8–10 NIV).

Jesus not only rebuked Satan for offering Him the political option, but He also rebuked His own disciples when they failed to understand His mission. Consider Matthew 16:21–26 where Jesus rebukes Peter:

> From that time on Jesus began to explain to his disciples that he must go to Jerusalem and suffer many things at the hands of the elders, chief priests and teachers of the law. And that he must be killed and on the third day be raised to life. Peter took him aside and began to rebuke him. "Never, Lord!" he said. "This shall never happen to you!" Jesus turned and said to Peter, "Out of my sight, Satan! You are a stumbling block to me; you do not have in mind the things of God, but the things of men." Then Jesus said to his disciples, "If anyone would come after me, he must deny himself and take up his cross and follow me. For whoever wants to save his life will lose it, but whoever loses his life for me will find it. What good will it profit a man if he gains the whole world yet forfeits his soul? Or what can a man give in exchange for his soul?"(NIV)

We might also be reminded that when the mother of Zebedee's sons came to Jesus and asked that her sons be allowed to sit next to Him in his kingdom, Jesus made it clear that His kingdom was not a matter of political rule, but of service. Even at the time of his arrest, Jesus made it clear that He would not use His power to turn away from the cross (Matt. 26:53–54).

Jesus and Saving Faith

While the work of Jesus Christ was not limited to the individual redemption of human souls, that was His *primary* purpose in coming as God in human flesh. At the time of Jesus' conception and at the time of His entry into public ministry, it was clearly announced that the purpose of His coming was to redeem humankind from sin. In the visit to Joseph, the angel of the Lord said of Mary, "She will bring forth a Son, and you shall call His name Jesus, for He will save His people from their sins" (Matt. 1:21). John the Baptist proclaimed of Jesus as he came toward him,

"Behold! The Lamb of God who takes away the sin of the world!" (John 1:29).

Jesus understood that He had come into the world to save sinners. He did not draw back from making it clear that those who accepted Him would have everlasting life. Jesus plainly stated, "I am the way, the truth, and the life. No one comes to the Father except through Me" (John 14:6). He also made it clear that it was the love of God the Father that compelled Him to send His only begotten Son into the world to atone for human sin. The scripture speaks of the comprehensive nature of Christ's sacrifice: "He has appeared to put away sin by the sacrifice of Himself" (Heb. 9:26b).

Faith in Jesus as savior comes by "hearing, and hearing by the Word of God" (Rom. 10:17). The context of this verse is the question of saving faith (10:9 and 10:13). Paul asks several questions: "How shall they call on Him in whom they have not believed? And how shall they believe in Him of whom they have not heard? And how shall they preach unless they are sent?" The larger context is that saving faith is brought about through the proclamation and communication of the Gospel. There can be no saving faith apart from the Gospel being proclaimed.

A COMMITMENT TO PROCLAMATION

Bounds reminds us again of the essential importance of proclaiming the Gospel of Jesus Christ with the expectation that this action will bring transformation to the individual, to social systems and to the cultures of the world.

> It is not by accident that Protestantism has emphasized the priority of Gospel proclamation in historic doctrinal standards. This emphasis is grounded in the public ministry of Jesus, the commission given by Christ to His disciples and in the practice of the early Church. Proclamation is the primary means by which the Kingdom of God is advanced in the world. Christ works through the Church's proclamation to create in people's lives the reality described in it.
>
> The United Methodist Church in her mission and ministry, in the recovery of her social witness must once again commit herself to

the task of preaching the "Word of God," of proclaiming the Gospel. While proclamation is not the only means by which God's redeeming and transforming grace is made available in the world, it is central. True social change . . . cannot happen apart from sharing the Gospel.[16]

Chapter Three
A Breakdown in Mission and Ministry

Pip: Your teachings were based fully upon Scripture and upon the Christian beliefs of those who went before you. But as times change, isn't it necessary for Christian doctrine to adjust to fit the culture in which we live?

Wesley: If you mean do the essential truths change, then let me draw from my statements on natural philosophy and say that we can neither depend upon reason nor experiment [experience]. Whatsoever men know or can know . . . must be drawn from the oracles of God. Here, therefore, we are to look for no new improvement; but to stand in the good old paths; to content ourselves with what God has been pleased to reveal; with "the faith once delivered to the saints."[1]

Pip: That is a most enlightening statement, given the current emphasis within Methodism on the importance of Scripture, tradition, reason, and experience in shaping our theology. These four guidelines have been called the "Wesleyan Quadrilateral," and are included in the current *Book of Discipline* as important in formulating our theology.

The *Discipline* states, "Wesley believed that the living core of the Christian faith was revealed in Scripture, illumined by tradition, vivified in personal experience, and confirmed by reason." Would you concur with this claim?

Wesley: This is a somewhat unusual belief to be attributed to me since I did not make this kind of clear delineation myself. I am not in disagreement with the statement as such, but would recommend caution if these four elements are to be considered equal in forming beliefs. I want to know one thing—the way to heaven. I want to know how to land safely on that happy shore. God himself has descended to teach the way; it is for this very purpose that Christ came from heaven. He has written the way in a book, O, give me that book! At any price give me the Book of God! I have it, and it contains knowledge enough for me. Let me be *homo unius libri*—a man of one book. . . . I have set down what I find in the Bible concerning the way to heaven. I am concerned to distinguish God's way from all human inventions. I have tried to describe true, scriptural, experiential religion so as to omit nothing that is a genuine part of it. I add not one thing to it that is not a vital component.[2]

THE SOCIAL GOSPEL AND THEOLOGICAL LIBERALISM

A Developing Gospel and Social Witness

As we examine our social witness, it is important to recall that the Gospel in Wesley's day was very personal and also promoted a dynamic social agenda that brought social reform. There were strong efforts for social justice—such as prison reform, child labor laws and societies for the poor. Likewise, in the mid-1800s, there was a very reform-minded Wesleyan movement in America. As in Wesley's England, Methodism in America had a vigorous social ministry which was a natural outgrowth of what was known as the Holiness Movement. Christians grew in personal and social holiness following their commitment to Christ.

The evangelical, Christian, social witness during the eighteenth and early nineteenth centuries of such individuals as John and Charles Wesley, George Whitfield, and their colleagues was made real as they worked tirelessly for prison reform, education, and medical care for the poor—even as they preached the Gospel and led individuals to faith in Christ as their *primary* focus. Likewise, in the nineteenth century, the holiness movement converted many people with a strong gospel message combined with a vibrant social witness. This is clear from the revivalists' work and influence on the abolition of slavery, temperance, and efforts on behalf of the poor. Timothy L. Smith said: "To be sure, politics never became the principal business of the evangelistic pulpit. . . . But, the nineteenth-century soul winners were at war with all sin."[3]

British and American Holiness Movement

Attempting to counter theological liberalism, the Holiness Movement was a call to re-adhere to Wesleyan principles and traditional theology. A return to revivalism and camp meetings emphasized sanctification through the baptism of the Holy Spirit.[4] These Methodists sought to preserve the message and the methods that had inspired the early itinerants and their converts and led to the phenomenal growth of Methodism in the first half of the nineteenth century. The holiness movement originated in the 1830s with Phoebe Palmer and Sarah Langford and their Tuesday Meeting for the Promotion of Holiness. Palmer and Langford modeled a truly Wesleyan social witness. This had a great impact on Methodism.[5]

Dr. Elaine Heath wonders how Palmer, Methodist evangelist and social activist of the nineteenth century, would respond to our often fragmented vision of evangelism and social witness today. "Palmer believed that the primary reason the world resisted evangelism was the absence of holiness in lukewarm Christians whom she castigated as biblically illiterate 'professors.'"[6]

There was a lot of cross-fertilization between the American and British holiness movements. In the second half of the nineteenth century, the American holiness movement spread to England and had a great impact upon the British. People associated with the American holiness movement, like Phoebe Palmer and Hannah Smith, lectured in England with great success. This helped give birth to the Keswick movement in England, which then spread to America. These social reform movements in England and in America were an expression of the vigorous, spiritual life of the evangelical revival era.

Movements that began in England, such as the Young Men's Christian Association (YMCA) and Salvation Army, expanded to America, and America grew its own holiness leaders and ministries, such as:

Women's Rights Movement/Evangelical Feminism:

- The establishment of Oberlin College as the first co-educational college in the world. Oberlin came out of and was an expression of the holiness movement, particularly of Charles Finney and Asa Mahon. Women were educated with men in the liberal arts.[7]

- Frances Willard, a Methodist crusader, used the Women's Temperance Union as an outlet to make women's suffrage "palatable to the masses."[8] In 1888, she also argued for the ordination of women in the pulpit.

- The nineteenth-century holiness movement opened new vistas for women in ministry. This was seen particularly in the work and ministry of Catherine Booth in the Salvation Army. In 1880, William Booth sent George Scott Railton, Captain Emma Westbrook, and six women soldiers to the Greater New York area to establish The Salvation Army in America. Their work grew quickly.[9]

- Lee Anna Starr, a Methodist Protestant pastor at Adrian College, authored *The Bible Status of Women* (1926). The book was published by Revell, the evangelical publisher associated with the Moody revivals.[10]

Gospel to the Poor:

- B. T. Roberts, who founded the Free Methodist Church, insisted Christians renounce such social sins as "slavery, driving hard bargains, and oppressing the hireling in his wages."[11]

- A. B. Simpson, founder of the Christian and Missionary Alliance, organized the group to serve the "neglected classes, both at home and abroad."[12]

- This era saw the establishment of seventy-five Florence Crittendon homes to work with women often involved in prostitution—educating them, helping with children, and training for jobs.[13]

- The Salvation Army, though primarily concerned with salvation and preaching the Gospel to the poor, soon found itself providing other services. Most immediate were the needs for food, clothing, and shelter. A "poor man's bank" was established. Day care centers were provided to permit mothers to get out and earn a living for their families. The Army discovered that the legal system was biased toward those who could afford to hire counsel, and it therefore provided free legal aid. Special attention was given to work among prisoners. The Army sought to become the custodian of first offenders to prevent them from being sent to prisons that would turn them into hardened criminals.[14]

There is no doubt that evangelicals were leaders in early social movements. The preaching of the Gospel was paramount—and a strong social witness was close behind. Smith writes:

> The experience of evangelicals in co-operative benevolent and missionary enterprises was rapidly awakening a new sense of responsibility for those whom a soulless industrial system had thrown upon the refuse heap of the city's slums. . . . Thus declined the ancient distinctions between piety and moralism, spiritual and social service.[15]

The balance between the proclamation of the Gospel and social witness Wesley and the holiness movement so beautifully exemplified has not always been achieved.

Dire Social Conditions Require a Response

The late nineteenth and early twentieth centuries brought even more societal changes. In a relatively short period of time America transitioned from an agrarian society to an industrial one. People left their small communities and moved to find work in the factories. Large cities grew up around the factories and immigrants from the farms and abroad crowded into tenements which frequently lacked running water or basic sanitation. The conditions in the factories were sometimes dangerous and often oppressive. Men, women, and children were forced into the workplace, where they worked for little pay; there was no way to address or improve their living conditions.

> The message of personal salvation through Christ gave way to a message of salvation through the advancement of culture.

The churches were not silent. They called the industrialized capitalist spirit into accountability. They did this in two ways: They called for Christians to reassess their lifestyles and for government to regulate industry for the benefit of the workers.[16]

In 1907, Walter Rauschenbusch published *Christianity and the Social Crisis*. It promoted a theological earthquake called the social gospel, a doctrine that placed the emphasis on liberal social change rather than evangelism. Rauschenbusch absorbed socialist writings of his day as he sought answers to severe social disorders during his twelve-year pastorate in the slums of New York City. He did not invent the social gospel, but his best-selling book ushered in a new era in Christian thought and action.[17]

The social gospel sought to transform social and governmental systems to create a more just world. It diminished the dimension of personal sin and alienation from God, and focused more on Christianizing society and bringing the Kingdom on earth. The social gospel emphasized the material rather than the spiritual needs of humanity.

Many of the social gospel preachers were mostly orthodox in their Christianity and did not embrace socialism in order to address the injustices of the early industrial movement. In fact, some preachers, while concerned with addressing the injustices of unbridled capitalism, were equally disturbed by certain aspects of the socialist movement. They warned the church against adopting socialist principles that were contrary to clear Christian teaching.

Nevertheless, for most advocates of the social gospel, the ideology of socialism became indistinguishable from their message. For the more radical, the social gospel redefined salvation as social progress. The message of personal salvation though Christ gave way to a message of salvation through the advancement of culture. The unjust treatment of factory workers and the excesses of capitalism had been brought into the light, but many in the mainline churches moved beyond the call for justice to the call for full acceptance of socialist ideology.

With this socialist ideology came other secular influences. These secular influences included the evolutionary worldview of Darwin, the work of Freud, and trends in philosophy that stressed the ethical and social aspects of Christianity, to the neglect of its personal aspects.

John Dewey is just one example of many intellectuals who advocated for the social gospel. In his book *A Common Faith*, he encouraged his followers to exchange traditional religion for the socialist struggle. Dewey was also instrumental in the formulation of "The Humanist Manifesto" (1933) which was hostile to American Christianity. Much hope was placed in socialism's capacity to address the excesses of capitalism and the plight of the poor. The socialist ideology became equated with the social gospel message—as expressed by Paul Tillich: "Any serious Christian must be a socialist."[18]

The Rise of Theological Liberalism

Another development was the onset of theological liberalism. Methodism, as well as other mainline denominations, felt the impact of theological liberalism in its seminaries, courses of study, and publications. The social gospel and theological liberalism emerged about the same time and interacted with each other. While they were, in a sense, two different movements, the social gospel reflected and was encouraged by theological liberalism. It was natural for one to embrace the social gospel and its focus on meeting human need because theological liberalism denied human sin and proposed that humanity was basically good. People did not need to be converted, but rather simply needed a better environment and more educational opportunities. It was thought if social conditions were changed for the better, it would help fan the flames of inherent goodness.

As it made inroads into the American church scene, the belief in inherent human goodness marginalized the church's teaching on sin and evil. Other basic tenets of historic Christianity—the virgin birth, atonement, resurrection, ascension, and Christ's promised return were sidelined as well, or sometimes denied.

This was due in part to the emergence of a new science that claimed all events could be explained by universal laws of cause and effect, leaving no room for unique events, divine revelation, or the supernatural. Rather, it insisted that all data should be tested empirically. This sweeping new worldview was devastating to the church's teaching authority because it brought into question all of the supernatural dimensions of the Gospel message.

Many who embraced these theological innovations believed they were helping preserve traditional Christianity by making it relevant or believable for modern, scientific man. Theologian Kenneth Kantzer said that religious liberalism was an attempt to update "an old beloved religion so it could survive the modern world." What was clear is that the church lost its confidence in the robust, clear, supernatural teachings of the Biblical message.

Many social gospel advocates tried to hold onto evangelical faith while becoming aggressive in social ministry. In time, however, the liberal theology that was becoming increasingly accepted in all American seminaries won the day. In a scientific era, the supernatural elements of the Gospel had to be played down or even removed; the emphasis was more on the ethics of the Gospel and the teachings of Jesus in the Sermon on the Mount. Jesus was the example, but not as atoning sacrifice for sin. Added to this was the influx of German

Rationalism, which rejected many of the basic tenets of the Christian faith in favor of "higher criticism." Higher criticism, arising from nineteenth-century European rationalism, generally takes a secular approach asking questions regarding the origin and composition of the biblical text. The principles of higher criticism are based on reason rather than revelation.

Heidinger applies the social gospel threat to Methodism:

> If we are ever to recover our theological identity, we must first understand what we have lost, when we lost it and how we lost it. If we have experienced defection from our basic Wesleyan doctrines, we need to know when it happened. To do this we must begin by examining what is known as the social gospel era, usually dated from the 1890s to the 1930s. This was a period of major transition and theological decline for Methodism. Though it seems far removed from us today, this was an era whose long shadow of influence still touches today's church.[19]

THE EFFECT UPON THE METHODIST CHURCH

The Christian Church at large reeled under the influence of the social gospel and theological liberalism. Over an extended period, the Church fought this rising tide, winning some battles, losing others. Some denominations opted to withdraw from the public arena and maintain doctrinal integrity by holding onto the fundamentals of the faith. Others, like the Methodist Church, suffered the incursion of liberal teaching in church-related seminaries, producing a clergy and denominational leadership in full sympathy with the emerging social teachings.[20]

Within Methodism, some sought to maintain Wesleyan distinctives such as the doctrine of Christian Perfection. Tension mounted between those who were unwilling to let go of what Wesley referred to as Methodism's *grand depositum*, and some who were more than ready to deny the church's traditional doctrine. The 1894 General Conference felt it must speak to the problem of independently operating holiness evangelists. Within six years, no less than ten separate religious bodies coming out of the Holiness Movement were organized.

Methodism lost a large number of holiness advocates—and it also lost its enthusiasm for debate over doctrinal issues.

Heidinger describes the result of this unfortunate situation:

> Increasingly [Methodists] boasted that they were not a doctrinal church. In this respect, Methodist theologians were in the process of denying their own relevance. . . . The new intellectual currents challenged Methodism's most basic Christian doctrines—revelation, the nature of man, sin, salvation, and eschatology.[21]

In 1908, there arose concern even among some of the progressive, more liberal-minded churchmen that something unhealthy was taking place with this new emphasis. One spokesman was Herbert Welch, the president of Ohio Wesleyan University and later a bishop of the Methodist Episcopal Church. Though in full sympathy with the emerging social teachings, Welch wrote:

> The peril is not that there may be too earnest an agitation of social needs, but that on one side should be a group of evangelists with a narrow conception of Christ's mission, intense in zeal, but lacking vision, breadth, adaptation to the needs and ways of the day; on the other a group of social workers, alive to the injustice of the present situation, aflame with love to men and the desire to bring in the kingdom of righteousness and peace, but distrusting the method of evangelism and substituting Utopia for heaven.[22]

Francis J. McConnell, an advocate of the social gospel who later became a Methodist bishop, expressed a fear that something was being lost from the Christian preaching to the individual:

> We concede that much preaching of the social gospel today does encourage a false belittling of the function of the individual. Some social leaders sneer at the doctrine of personal salvation as old-fashioned and proclaim that if we get the right group spirit the salvation of the individuals will take care of itself.[23]

Some continued to protest that the fundamental, basic doctrines in Methodism were being either neglected or modified, if not abandoned. Some of the strongest protest came from Harold Paul Sloan, a prominent pastor in the New Jersey Conference. He was the founder of The Methodist League for Faith and Life, a movement one might call the Good News movement of the 1920s.[24]

The Methodist League for Faith and Life gained a large following, including the support of Bishop Adna W. Leonard. However, as momentum grew, Bishop Leonard distanced himself from the movement, giving heartbreak to the renewalists and hurting the call for doctrinal faithfulness.

As the church faced many, new complex issues brought about by industrialization and urbanization, there might have been a successful joining of the Gospel and social witness in the sense of reclaiming what John Wesley had effectively defined and practiced since the inception of the Methodist movement—however, this did not happen.

Despite the impact of the social gospel and theological liberalism on Methodism during the early twentieth century, the message and the hymnody of Methodism has remained intact in the hearts and minds of the laity and of evangelical clergy. If you look at polls regarding Methodist beliefs, about 65 percent will call themselves theologically conservative and will hold a conservative understanding of the Bible.

THE FUNDAMENTALIST BACKLASH

By the early twentieth century, there was a deep concern that the social gospel was taking the church far from the fundamentals of Christian faith. Unable or unwilling to confront the scientific, secular, and political challenges, many fundamentalists turned away from the controversies within the mainstream culture. They concentrated on creating a Christian counterculture. In this regard, they did much to preserve the basic teachings of historic Christian orthodoxy. They were active in missions and Bible studies, maintained soup kitchens, and founded schools and seminaries. The work of these Christians, however, went largely unnoticed, mainly because the activism of the time was moving in a socialist direction.

Interpreting "Fundamentalism"

When some people hear the word "fundamentalism," they associate it with a closed mind that refuses to engage the culture and take social injustice seriously. Some of the criticism centers on the fundamentalist's view of the end times, the imminent return of Christ as well as the "understanding of the Bible that divides the relationship of God to humanity into sharply separated epochs (dispensations)."[25] But blanket applications cannot be made to fundamentalists any more than other groups. Mark Noll, in *The Scandal of the Evangelical Mind*, acknowledges that some fundamentalists created problems for Christian intellectual development. But he also makes an important point in their defense:

> Fundamentalists of the early twentieth century defended many convictions essential to a traditional understanding of Christianity. At a time when naturalism threatened religion, when relativism assaulted social morality, when intellectual fashions were turning the Bible into a book of merely antiquarian interest, fundamentalists said what needed to be said about the supernatural character of religion, the objectivity of Christian morality, and the timeless validity of Scripture.[26]

During the 1970s, conservative evangelicals launched a movement dedicated to restoring traditional values to public policy. These evangelical, often fundamentalist, Christians became known as the "Christian Right." A host of separate reactions to cultural liberalism originated from this group, including the battle to prevent state ratification of the Equal Rights Amendment; a bitter controversy over school textbooks in Kanawah County, West Virginia; a gay rights referendum in Dade County, Florida; and a series of "I Love America" rallies conducted on statehouse steps by Jerry Falwell. These culture wars became commonplace in the 1980s and 1990s, including fights over schools, abortion, public expression of religion, and gay rights. This activism shows no signs of abating.[27]

It is important to distinguish between what has become known as the fundamentalist movement and proponents of the fundamentals of the faith. Fundamentalists in the first half of the twentieth century sometimes overreacted to the theological liberalism, socialist leanings, and political activism which became a hallmark in the work of the National Council of Churches. At the same time, they were understandably concerned that the Gospel and the teachings of Scripture be preserved. Also, some fundamentalist groups were skeptical of suggested social remedies. While some may have overreacted and proposed extreme responses, others recognized the need to remain faithful to the fundamental doctrines of the Christian faith. Often, the term "fundamentalist" is thrown out in a vague and invective manner. In our own United Methodist denomination, there are those who call the church to be faithful to core doctrines and who challenge fashionable, trendy theological proposals on both the right and the left. It is inaccurate to label these individuals or groups "fundamentalists" in the negative sense of the word.

John Wesley and the Fundamentals

Wesley refused to battle over opinion, and went out of his way to find common ground with those who differed with him.[28] Wesley based his sermon, "Catholic spirit," on a verse found in 2 Kings: "If your heart is right with my heart then take my hand"(10:15). Yet, in this same sermon, Wesley made it clear Methodists were not to be "driven to and fro, and tossed about with every wind of doctrine." Wesley stated that those of a catholic spirit should be "fixed as the sun in his judgment concerning the main branches of Christian

Wesley refused to battle over opinion, and went out of his way to find common ground with those who differed from him.

doctrine."[29] There is no doubt that Wesley held to certain fundamental doctrines. A list of doctrines that were considered essential
by Wesley included: original sin, the deity of Christ, the atonement,
justification by faith alone, the work of the Holy Spirit (including
new birth and holiness), and the Trinity.[30] Repentance also appears
in other references. One might say that Wesley was a "fundamentalist" in the finest sense of the term.

FINDING OUR WAY

When we confuse the scripturally revealed Gospel of Jesus
Christ with a substituted human invention, the "social gospel," there
is a breakdown in mission and ministry. When this occurs, some
come to believe that bearing social witness or doing social justice
is the Gospel. Others recoil at the very idea of social ministry
altogether. Neither of these positions represents the Biblical,
Wesleyan ministry model. Our goal is to navigate between these two
unbiblical extremes within the church today.

We can be assured that Wesley would be in agreement with those
who hold to the fundamentals of Christian faith. He challenged
theological viewpoints that he felt were contrary to Biblical teaching
in his writings. We can be equally assured that he understood social
ministry to be subservient to preaching the Gospel, yet, intimately
linked to it.

Chapter Four
Present-Day Liberalism and Conservatism

Pip: What's the difference between Christian ethics and cultural ethics?

Wesley: Christian ethics, or theological ethics, is based on the conclusions of a religious outlook, on a distinctly biblical world-view. Cultural, or philosophical ethics, pertains to the present life. Christian ethics is concerned about both the present life and the life after death.[1]

Pip: Is there a foundation for Christian ethics?

Wesley: Christian theology starts with the Creator, not the created. "In the beginning God created" is where we begin. From there we understand that All Christian ethics are based upon God's work within us to make us holy in heart and life. I myself begin with regeneration and justification as I wrote: "All works done before justification are not good, in the Christian sense, forasmuch as they spring not of faith in Jesus Christ . . . they are not done as God hath willed and commanded them to be done, we doubt not . . . but they have the nature of sin."[2]

Pip: Are there other Christian principles you would offer that will aid us in our day?

Wesley: Well, I might add, it will take our cooperation with God if we are to realize our redemption and if we are to do good works.

God works in you; therefore, you must work. You must be "workers together with him" . . . otherwise he will cease working.[3] God alone enables us to repent, turn from sin, trust in the merits of Christ, and live holy lives.[4]

Pip: Once we have come to this place of faith, how are we to live holy lives in a decadent culture?

Wesley: Some think the moral law does not have to be kept since Christ paid the penalty for our sins—others believe their good works add to their salvation. Both of these understandings are false. On the one hand, the law continually makes way for, and points us to, the gospel; on the other hand, the gospel continually leads us to a more exact fulfilling of the law.[5] If the fulfilling of the moral law is both necessary and possible, God expects us to discipline ourselves to obey its commands and benefit from its promises.[6]

Pip: Now it seems we are moving toward applying our Christian ethics to our daily living. Do I hear another principle in your final statement? Is there more?

Wesley: You hear well. The principle of disciplined living is one the people called Methodist came to be known for. In all my writings, I urged my hearers to place service ahead of creature comforts and to prioritize duty over personal convenience.[7] This way of living is possible only by self-denial, which I called a "grand doctrine of Christianity."[8]

Is there more, you ask? There is one more ethical principal I must pass on to you. My keystone of personal and social ethics is *love*. I consider this the epitome of religion and the sum of Christian perfection as stated by our Lord, "You shall love the Lord your God with all your heart, and with all your soul, and with all your mind. This is the greatest and first commandment. And a second is like it: You shall love your neighbor as yourself. On these two commandments hang all the law and the prophets" (Matt. 22:37–40).[9]

OUTGROWTHS OF THEOLOGICAL LIBERALISM

As we think of our complex world and the far-reaching issues we must address as Christians, we might not have expected the kind of principles or theological ethics John Wesley held in his day to be so relevant to ours. And yet, they are right on target. After all, his day was as complex as our own in many ways—and humans are not so changed.

Modern-day liberalism is a by-product of the social gospel and theological liberalism movements. Liberalism, like conservatism, covers a broad spectrum of held beliefs. Among both liberals and conservatives, there are those who self-identify as "moderate," meaning they do not hold the hard lines of either category.

More hard-core liberalism champions a worldview including Marxism, socialism, liberation theology, universalism, radical feminism, social welfare, and wealth redistribution.

A look at some of these systems will help us understand the right motivations that often produced wrong outcomes.

By the second half of the twentieth century it was clear that the social gospel had failed to deliver on its objectives to minister to the community, evangelize the social order, and bring the kingdom of God on earth by way of social justice. Dallas Willard has said that liberal theology found itself ". . . bludgeoned to its knees by world events, its intellectual capacity exhausted, and incapable of providing concepts that could clarify exactly what was happening in Western life and society at the time . . ."[10] Much hope had been placed in political reform, social progress, and scientific advantages. There are many reasons they did not succeed, the most significant of which was the denial of the supernatural aspects of the historic Gospel.

Furthermore, the social gospel was frequently allied with Marxist ideology—an ideology that would ultimately prove to be not only insufficient to bring about desired social change, but also sustainable only under the most oppressive, coercive, totalitarian means. Everywhere the Marxist model was tried, it proved to be a failure. The church must take a long look at where these ideologies have impacted our theology.

Early Civil Rights Movement

The early civil rights movement was one of the most successful struggles for social justice in the twentieth century. What began as a cry for basic human decency opened the eyes of the church, country, and world to racially motivated bigotry and discrimination. The larger principles of brotherly love and Christ's call to love our neighbor as ourselves had long been neglected as it applied to racism. The civil rights movement brought about much-needed social reform. But more important, it focused the world on a deficit of the heart and challenged society in strong religious terms to deal with the sin of racism.

Those who participated in the marches and demonstrations testify to their sense of godly purpose and of faithfulness to the first and second commandments. For some, the activism itself was viewed as transformative and the very reason for belief. For many, social action took the place of personal salvation—or supplanted it in importance.[11] The early appeal to Christians of all races to open their eyes and hearts to a real breakdown of holiness and love of neighbor was largely lost in the themes of liberation and redistribution of power. But for all its social reform brought about by the civil rights movement, it was not able to rid this country of the evil of racism.

Liberation Theology

At the same time the civil rights movement was sweeping across North America, another liberation movement was emerging. In 1971, the release of Gustavo Gutierrez's electrifying book *A Theology of Liberation* brought liberation theology to the forefront in Latin America and beyond. Like the social gospel movement, this movement sought to address the very real problems of the poor and marginalized in Latin America, Asia, and South Africa. Black Americans were also included. Many of these problems were the result of poor government policies that failed to address malnutrition, health care, and basic human services. Added to this was military torture and the cruel treatment of innocent people. Economic exploitation by outside interests contributed to the plight of the poor. In the liberationist view, God is at work in the efforts of humanity to change society. Salvation is achieved through political and economic struggles that bring liberation from oppression. Christ's death is viewed as an ongoing working out of God's plans for humanity and the world through human effort. Particularly in liberation theology, the suffering of the poor is considered as having saving merit, eliminating the need for salvation through Christ. Those who stand in solidarity with the poor also reap spiritual benefits. Sin is viewed as systemic, rather than within the individual.

The theological left[12] took up these themes and the message of Christ became, for many, the struggle against oppression. Separating salvation from Christ's work on the cross to a general concept of social justice and liberation meant people could unite behind a multitude of causes that do not require faith in God or Christ. This error is a classic example of a half-truth, for the Scriptures speak mightily of God's concern for the poor and oppressed. The problem is that the liberationist view neglects the fact of the oppression of human sin. Sadly, in many cases where this theology was applied, one type of oppression was exchanged for another.

An additional major criticism of liberation theology was the acceptance of violence to achieve the desired end results. Equally troubling was its departure from Scripture and the substitution of Marxist principles of revolutionary political action.

The problem is that the liberationist view neglects the fact of the oppression of sin.

Radical Feminism

Feminism sprang from legitimate concerns that women were not experiencing equality with men in society and in the workforce. As with the civil rights movement and liberation theology, the feminist movement became politicized and fragmented into various forms of feminism, some of which represented legitimate interests with reasoned arguments and some which became radicalized. In his article "Feminism and Feminism," Richard John Neuhaus gave clarity to the various branches of feminism:

> Liberal feminism is straightforward. It insists that women have a right to fair treatment and equal opportunity in trying to realize their aspirations. Gender feminism, on the other hand, claims that our entire social and cultural order is skewed by the "hegemony" of a patriarchal sex/gender system that is designed to oppress and exploit women. Gender feminism claims to be and is radical in its attempt to overthrow that putative system by consciousness raising and revolutionary action.[13]

In her book *The Feminist Gospel*, Mary Kassian identifies a link between liberation theology and feminist theology. Kassian addresses the theological aspects of radical feminism. She writes:

> Feminist theologians saw many parallels between the condition of the Latin American people and the condition of women. . . . Feminist scholars claimed that the domination of women by men was "the most ancient and persistent form of the subjection of one human being to a permanent status of inferiority because of sex." . . . Feminist theologians believed that the liberation of women would induce the end of poverty, racial discrimination, ecological destruction, and war. They argued that it would end all dualisms, usher in a new world order of peace, and witness the birth of a new humanity.[14]

For all its idealism, feminist theology soon moved far beyond a biblical worldview. Early feminists questioned the doctrines of God, Jesus, salvation, redemption, sin, ecclesiology, and eschatology. They found much in them to be incompatible with the feminist paradigm of liberation and equality, and, therefore, revised traditional doctrinal definitions to fit the feminist vision.

Radical feminists also changed the traditional understanding of Church, viewing the Church as existing for the purpose of bringing liberation by overthrowing the oppressive structures within society.

While not all feminists embraced this radical theology, some did accept it in all areas of their lives. A counter-Christian worldview emerged regarding marriage, family, abortion, and homosexual practice, to name a few.

NCC and WCC Involvement

The National Council of Churches and the World Council of Churches organizes its work around activist causes and issues of liberation, economic equality, and social justice. The ecumenical movement helped define the original purpose of the NCC. A major focus of their initial purpose was to promote Christian unity by bringing together different Christian communions to share their mutual confession of Jesus Christ as Savior and Lord and their understanding of the Gospel as revealed in Scripture. From this good beginning, the NCC moved toward uniting the Christian community around activist causes, beginning with the civil rights movement and later moving on to include the protest of the Vietnam War, women's liberation, environmental justice, and a host of other issues.[15] Many leaders in United Methodist boards and agencies became part of the leadership of the NCC.

The activist posture of the National Council of Churches begun in the civil rights movement was taken up by the World Council of Churches. Through the late 1960s and into the 1970s, the WCC represented the causes of liberation and social justice.[16]

IN SEARCH OF SOCIAL JUSTICE

Both the social gospel and theologies of liberation have impacted our working definition of "social justice." Generally, social justice claims that societies can be as virtuous as individuals, or can adopt laws and social policies that favor the least in society and minimize harm.

Social justice comes with certain political and ideological commitments about how the church should minister to the poor and care for the marginalized of society. It is often at the very point that ideology is introduced that the church loses its way.[17] It is not always easy to distinguish between mere ideologies and biblical principles. A good example of a widely accepted ideology is the adaptation of Marxism by liberationists who see every social problem as a struggle between the oppressor and the oppressed. Sound theology is crucial to the church's search for social justice today.

The Gospel of Christ ultimately becomes secondary to this ideology and is eventually marginalized or abandoned altogether. Work may still be done in the name of Christ and on behalf of the Gospel. But the social witness itself does not rely on the Gospel as integral to ministry.

A common denominator in both the social gospel and liberation theology is a commitment to socialist principles. Another is viewing sin and salvation as not individual, but collective—that is, to social groups, systems, and institutions that embody and promote such sins. The individual becomes a victim, and some argue that being sinned against by the system releases the victim from any personal responsibility.

Sound theology is crucial to the church's search for social justice today.

In 1998, Richard Rorty summed up this ideological commitment in *Achieving Our Country: Leftist Thoughts in Twentieth-Century America*. He says that the commitment to social justice defines the left, and social justice is defined by the redistribution of wealth by the government.[18] There is an interesting paradox here. The goal of liberation is lost when individual freedom is sacrificed for an understanding of social justice which is committed ideologically to redistribution of wealth or power. This is not achievable except through coercion.

Of course we should recognize that this is a utopian goal that has not proven to be achievable. Thomas Oden puts it powerfully:

> The Marxist-Leninism of the Soviet era is now gone. The Freudian idealization of sexual liberation has found it easier to make babies than parent them. The children of today's culture are at peril. The idealized modernity they expected has never arrived, and its fantasy has left a trail of devastation. These once-assured ideologies are now unmasked as having a dated vision of the human possibility. None have succeeded in fashioning a transmissible intergenerational culture.[19]

Society is done no favor when the church bases its stand for justice on failed ideologies, untried political schemes, or untested scientific theories. When the church ties its understanding of social justice to political commitments, it loses its way. Almost without exception, the point where the church becomes impotent and irrelevant is the point at which it allows politically driven ideologies to define its mission in the social realm.

Some Methodists say that the social witness programs of our boards and agencies or the NCC or WCC are partisan and politically left-leaning. If social justice is to have any real meaning within the church, it must be freed from ideological, partisan, political commitments. Oden makes the point:

> They [North American Mainline] are locked into political agendas mandated neither by Scripture nor by ecumenical tradition. They have thrown themselves into partisan or utopian crusades— pro-abortion politics, radical feminism, coercive state regulatory practices, desperate and frustrated anti-globalization activism, statist dependency politics, class warfare rhetoric, unscientific visions of environmentalism, and permissive sexual liberation. Where these well-intentioned causes have gone awry, they have inflicted serious damage upon both church and society.[20]

Does social justice have to be envisioned from the ideology of liberation through redistribution and its accompanying political commitments? Certainly not. If we are to reclaim a vibrant Wesleyan social witness, we must free our notion of social justice from the failed ideologies of the past and the political loyalties of the present. What we need is a new envisioning of social justice—free from the political vision of the old-line liberation/redistribution commitments. The twentieth-century ideal of social justice must be abandoned and a new understanding of social justice formulated.

Our Current Dilemma

The United Methodist Church is dealing with many problems created by neglecting our Wesleyan, scriptural heritage. This heritage encompasses both personal salvation and a social witness.

Delegates to General Conference will be asked to assess many legislative proposals. Some will relate to the *Discipline* and our theological task, others will address our mission, and still others will examine our social witness in the world. All of us as United Methodists live under the decisions made at General Conference. Our programs and resources will affect the prevailing worldview of our Church—either a biblical worldview or a natural worldview. The application of scriptural authority is critical to all that we are as a Church.

Neglect in preaching and teaching the core tenets of Christianity, as well as the acceptance of truth-distorting theological, social, and political constructs, destroys our witness in the world.

Legislative Action

The Book of Resolutions is a collection of all current and official social policies and other resolutions adopted by the General Conference of The United Methodist Church. The resolutions passed at General Conference give individuals—and particularly boards and agencies—approval for political positions and programs they want to promote. It is interesting to note that over 75 percent of the resolutions in the *2004 Book of Resolutions* were submitted by official church agencies, with 67 percent originating from the General Board of Church and Society, the General Board of Global Ministries, and the Women's Division.

We will not be taken seriously when real issues of justice arise and the Gospel goes missing.

While resolutions are not binding upon the general church, they are, as stated above, a primary source for program initiatives on the part of our boards and agencies, giving them the rightful claim of General Conference approval for specific program initiatives. Many of the programs, policies, and initiatives sanctioned in *The Book of Resolutions* are out of step with grassroots United Methodists. Actions taken by our boards and agencies affect both our credibility and our effectiveness. Hence the need to be very cautious when considering controversial or partisan legislation.

Some faithful United Methodists say it does not matter when UMC officials or boards and agencies make political pronouncements, because no one takes them seriously anyway. "Give them their resolutions," they say. "It makes them feel better." This is a dangerous way of thinking. There is much evidence that radical political actions contribute heavily toward membership loss. Besides, this thinking fails to acknowledge that many are genuinely offended by such activity—not to mention that a vast amount of denominational funds are used to justify any number of questionable policies that have nothing to do with the mission of the church. We will not be taken seriously when real issues of justice arise and the Gospel goes missing.

Christians of all persuasions must be careful "to distinguish God's way from all human inventions," as John Wesley so aptly said. As United Methodists, we must learn to differentiate between theological, political, and social ideas that are based on experience rather than on the revelation that the world is transformed by the power of God in Christ through the work of the Holy Spirit, and not through raw human effort.

Chapter Five

The State of the Church

Pip: The membership of The United Methodist Church has been in decline for the last thirty-nine years. Why do you think this is?

Wesley: That is distressing. Yet, I am not afraid that the people called Methodist should ever cease to exist either in Europe or America. But I am afraid, lest they should only exist as a dead sect, having the form of religion without the power.[1] How many of those who profess to believe the whole, yet, in effect, preach another gospel; so disguising the essential doctrines thereof, by their new interpretations, as to retain the words only, but nothing of "the faith once delivered to the saints"![2]

STARTING WELL

Methodists in America grew from fewer than 5,000 in 1776 to more than 130,000 in 1806.[3] But actually, the story begins even earlier. Despite strong resistance and persecution leveled at the Wesleys, Methodism took firm root in Ireland. "Irish Methodism became the parent of Methodism on the American continent. Two names stand out conspicuously among its founders—Robert Strawbridge from County Leitrim and Philip Embury from the Palatine community in County

Limerick."[4] Nor can we overlook Barbara Heck, Embury's cousin, who encouraged him to begin preaching in his own house in America, warning him that if he did not, "God will require our blood at your hands."[5]

Strawbridge, an itinerant lay preacher like Embury, settled at Sam's Creek in Maryland in the 1760s. There he shared the Gospel with his neighbors and they built The Log Meeting-House—the first Methodist preaching-house on the continent. When the first American Methodist Conference assembled in Philadelphia in 1773, almost half the total membership of 1,160 were converts under Strawbridge.[6]

Embury had settled in New York. In 1766, Wesley's Chapel was built in the city—most likely the first chapel called by Wesley's name.[7]

In 1768, at the plea for help from the American Methodists, John Wesley asked his preachers in Conference, "Who is willing to go?" The next year, Richard Boardman and Joseph Pilmoor responded. In 1771, twenty-six-year-old Francis Asbury answered the challenge. He eventually became the first American Bishop and would be known as the Father of American Methodism.

The first Methodist Conference in America took place in Baltimore, Maryland, on December 24, 1784, and is known in American Methodist history as the Christmas Conference. ". . . Few outside the city paid much heed to that assembly of some sixty Methodist preachers . . . Yet there and then decisions were recorded which influenced profoundly the future of religious and social life in the new Republic and far beyond."[8] Henry Carter writes:

> Wesley saw the world as his parish; and in unforeseen ways the testimony of the Evangelist of England, heard and responded to in Ireland, reached across the Atlantic, struck root, and grew in the course of two centuries into a Protestant Church whose membership is now numbered by millions.[9]

Taking Root and Growing

By 1850, one third of the entire church membership in America was Methodist.[10] What caused this root to grow and flower into a great denomination? Ignited by saving faith in Jesus Christ, and the gracious love of God and others, they knew the power of full redemption from ills of soul and body. Convinced that the Holy Spirit intervened supernaturally in human lives, their goal was to bring persons to saving faith, to be formed in holiness of heart and life. They knew God could remodel "the least and the lowest into new creations."[11] This was an attractive message for westward moving settlers encountering the harsh realities of a formidable American wilderness!

Certainly, a major factor in American Methodism's growth was the simplicity of the Gospel message which the Methodist evangelist sent to the emerging nation. Wesley claimed he preached "a plain religion for a plain people." Francis Asbury echoed Wesley when Methodist clergy and laity alike were criticized for their lack of formal education by saying, "a simple man can speak and write for simple, plain people, upon simple truths."[12]

The nineteenth century has been called the Methodist Age by some historians because of the incredible success of Methodist circuit preachers who took the simple Gospel message into the American frontier. Suffering extreme privations, these unselfish and resolute riders pursued settlers into the remotest regions of the west.

Methodist and other evangelists held revivals, often in tents, and converted many through simple Biblical evangelical appeal. In *The Churching of America 1776–2005*, authors Roger Finke and Rodney Stark note that church growth was made possible by the work of itinerant preachers who ministered to relatively small groups of believers. They attribute the unquestioned success of the itinerant clergy to their preaching of the Gospel, which was motivated by the saving of souls, not material comfort.

> Indeed, it would be hard to imagine that any sum of money could have motivated Bishop Asbury to travel nearly 300,000 miles on horseback and by carriage, disregarding weather and chronic ill-health, to supervise his far-flung network of itinerants and circuit riders.[13]

Records of early annual conferences from 1780 to 1860 show that growth for black membership mirrored the growth of white membership.[14] There were black Methodist evangelists as early as

1780.[15] Tensions between the races led to the formation of African Methodist denominations, particularly following the Civil War. It can be said, however, that perhaps more than any denomination, the Methodists were concerned for the salvation of black Americans and purposed to share their faith with them.

Methodist itinerant clergy also organized local churches and set up class meetings to encourage spiritual growth in their absence.[16] Settlers encouraged, exhorted, reproved, and comforted one another in the faith. These early class meetings increased understanding of the essentials of the faith, and the tight connection of fellowship was reinforced by disciplined membership and the active participation of lay leaders.

Methodism had spread in all directions with the growing nation. The future looked promising.

LOSING MOMENTUM

A Fractured Movement

But as early as 1850, some Methodists began to show concern that the church was drifting away from its historic teachings. Free Methodists charged that the church was no longer the church of the Wesleys or of Asbury. Other groups within the Methodist Episcopal Church eventually left. In 1904, G. W. Wilson wrote *Methodist Theology vs. Methodist Theologians*. In the book's introduction, Bishop Willard Mallalieu expressed regret and concern that the moral and theological standards of the church had been lowered to accommodate worldly behavior. In his words, American Methodism was becoming "unevangelical, un-Wesleyan and unscriptural."[17]

Finke and Stark report that between 1916 and 1926, the mainlines lost 5,631 churches; 3,185 were Methodist Episcopal churches.[18] During that same period, there was a net increase of 4,667 American churches. The authors conclude that the social gospel reformers of this era sought to replace the American evangelical spirit with a new principle of social service and social witness. Many, however, rejected this as a poor substitute to scriptural Christianity and as insufficient to meet the spiritual and social needs of the people.

The early social reformers attempted to organize and unify churches around social issues. They hoped this would address certain social concerns and bring needed reforms, but it was ultimately unsuccessful.

The fallout from this division continues to have long-range effects upon mainline churches today. We should learn the lesson that the early social reformers did not: for the church and its social witness to be successful, social action must flow out of nothing less than a commitment to share Christ with a hurting world.

Our Diluted Witness

Over three million have left what was America's largest denomination. Forty years ago, nearly one out of every fifteen Americans belonged to our denomination. Now it's about one out of every forty! In the entire course of Christian history, it is difficult to find precedent for this kind of decline.

Many who will read this book cherish a heritage that goes back several generations in the American Methodist movement. Others have been attracted to The United Methodist Church more recently. For all, disunity and membership loss is a concern. Where the message remains true to our Biblical, Wesleyan heritage, the people called Methodist continue to increase. When social justice activism trumps making disciples of Jesus Christ in our churches, membership declines.

MEMBERSHIP CHALLENGES

Loss of Membership

In the late 1980s, several bishops called attention to the decline in Methodism. Bishop Richard B. Wilke wrote, "The church is sick unto death." He called the church to refocus on Jesus and save souls from sin, suggesting, "Seminaries must fuel the faith of our new ministers."[19] Bishop Earl G. Hunt discussed a long list of challenges and issues that were confronting the church in his book *A Bishop Speaks His Mind*. William Willimon and Robert Wilson wrote *Rekindling the Flame*, in which they published this startling statistic:

"The United Methodist Church, in the fourteen-year period 1970–1984, lost an average of 1,930 members every week."[20] Statistics for 2005 from the Web site (www.gcfa.org/) of the United Methodist General Commission on Finance and Administration (GCFA), show a gain in professing membership only in the Southeastern Jurisdiction (USA); West Africa; Congo; Africa; and the Philippines Central Conferences.[21]

In 1968, the Methodist Episcopal Church merged with the Evangelical United Brethren, giving us The United Methodist Church. At the time of the merger, we had over eleven million members. We have since lost over three million members. This is a cataclysmic loss. While the church leadership seems unsure as to why we have experienced such loss, we are confident that thousands have left for other denominations and independent churches because of the liberal theology and partisan political/social involvement. We also know we haven't reached young people for several generations, thus the percentage of our membership between the ages of eighteen and thirty-five years of age is well below the percentage of total Americans in that age group. This is supported by numerous studies.

As early as 1972, Dean Kelly, an executive of the National Council of Churches wrote *Why Conservative Churches Are Growing*, in which he noted that the liberal and mainline churches were declining at the same time conservative, evangelical bodies were rapidly growing. Kelly made the observation that organizations that held high standards were stronger than those with more lenient ones, and he added "that the mainline churches were declining not because they asked too much of their members but because they asked too little."[22] Finke and Stark concluded that "costly religion" with high demands and distinctive boundaries leads to Christian vitality and growth, not away from it.[23]

Willimon and Wilson urged the church to look into deeper root issues, writing "The Gospel, rather than the needs of the world, defines the mission of the church. In fact, apart from the Gospel, the world does not know what it needs."[24] They wrote that our church speaks mostly in political rather than religious terms, which causes divisiveness since many of the laity find this objectionable.

Loss of Purpose

John Wesley's desire was that Methodists continue as a movement with spiritual power. How is this possible in light of religious and secular voices that speak with the intention of cooling spiritual fervor—or diverting it toward another gospel?

The UMC mission statement makes it clear that our primary purpose is to make disciples of Jesus Christ, and that this is done by proclaiming the good news of God's grace.

Distortion of Purpose

The purpose of the church has become confused. William Willimon wrote:

> The church serves the world and affects the wider society—by being the church . . . Rather than simply developing slogans about justice, we are to define Christian justice by our care of one another in the church. Rather than pleading with Congress to do right, we are to build a people of righteousness in our local congregations. This is how the church serves the world and affects the wider society.[25]

Willimon makes the case that early American Methodists and Evangelical United Brethren founded social institutions not for the benefit of society but to "preserve the integrity of the church." The integrity of the church serves society in a way that activism is simply not capable of doing—especially when that activism is based on social justice and not the radical righteousness to which Christ calls us.

In a very real sense, the integrity of the church reflects the integrity of the Gospel. Wesley insisted that our love of God was reflected in our love for one another. Wesley took the Gospel to the poor and addressed the social conditions of his day, not from a perspective of justice, but from a perspective of righteousness and love that flows from faith and obedience to God. Early Methodists were a people of visible righteousness who cared for each another and those around them. They modeled justice in all they did, based upon their commitment to Christ and his teachings. Tom Thomas linked this concept to justification and sanctification.

> When considering John Wesley's social witness, keep in mind Wesley's assumption "true religion" includes justification and sanctification together as the one, grand possibility for fully redeeming humankind from all evils, both of soul and body. Not just justification, or sanctification alone, but both joined working together in their proper relation, sequence, and place.[26]

The General Board of Higher Education and Ministry (GBHEM) consulted with membership, ecclesiology, and leadership early in 2007 to consider what the nature of the church is in terms of membership. In a paper prepared for the consultation, Rev. Leicester Longden called attention to the danger of confusing the political polity of American politics with the polity of the church. In other words, will we understand church polity as based on tolerance, or as "Baptism into *communion* by means of 'costly grace,' redemption from sin, power to live a new life, and a call to radical holiness?"[27]

This call for clarification goes to the heart of the nature and purpose of the church. The UMC most likely would not be having this debate if the concerns of righteousness, rather than a political perspective of justice, informed our understanding of the purpose of the church. The credibility of the church will inevitably suffer when its purpose is confused or clouded by political concerns. When our social witness becomes more about lobbying for political goals, it has profound effects on the understanding of the church's purpose and mission. Consider this thought from Richard John Neuhaus:

> The hunger for a truly satisfying way of putting the world in order is laudable. But that is a hunger for the kingdom of God, and it is dangerously misplaced when it is invested in the political arena.[28]

Loss of Credibility

The Church of Jesus Christ is to be God's faithful witness in the world. Think about the birth of the Church as described in the Book of Acts. What was the first occurrence after the infilling of the Holy Spirit? It was the proclamation of the Gospel to the multitudes by Peter. Three thousand were added to the church that day. Many miraculous and eventful things followed this initial formation of the church as the apostles and converts shared the Gospel, experienced the power of the Holy Spirit working through their ministries, and learned to live together in Christian community. It was only when sin and personal agendas surfaced that the church failed—and had to be brought back to the truths of the apostolic faith.

When the church fails in its vital mission, its witness suffers—in the lives of Christ's followers, in the eyes of the community, and in

> Early Methodists were a people of visible righteousness who cared for each other and those around them.

faithful testimony to the biblical model. The United Methodist Church has experienced such loss of credibility.

Individuals and groups have pointed to many episodes over the past forty years where misguided social activism has eroded our church's credibility in the eyes of members and in the Christian community. Indeed, polarizing political and social actions diminish our witness in the world and threaten our denomination. United Methodists have widely divergent opinions on political/social issues. Individuals within the church are praying and often leaving over these and other occurrences in the church. Recently, in her private devotions, a woman was reading from the book of Daniel, Chapter 9. She wrote in an e-mail:

> I first read Daniel's prayer in my old RSV Bible and there is a phrase that is repeated that seemed so amazingly accurate when I think about our church today. It is in verses 7 and 8: "To thee, O Lord,

belongs righteousness, but to us confusion of face. . . . " Can you think of a better way to describe the UM Church right now than "Confusion of Face"? In the NIV it is translated as "we are covered with shame" which is also good, but the other phrase really came out at me. When we talk or listen to people as they speak about our church it seems that we as a church have a "confusion of face" to people.[29]

How unfortunate that a faithful member of the church is so deeply concerned about the integrity of her denomination. How are we to re-establish our integrity among our own members, in the culture, and in the world? Willimon and Wilson answer:

The United Methodist Church must recover a sense of its own integrity as a distinct phenomenon in American society. Integrity implies boundaries, limits, a discernible identity and focus of activity. The church is more than a society to provide activities for its members, more than a platform for political agitation. The task of the church is much the same as the task Wesley gave to his societies: to form a community of faith and practice that responds, in its life together and witness to the world, to the presence of Jesus Christ. Formation of a visible people of God is the radical imperative preceding everything else the church is about. In a sense, the first "business" of the church is to be the church.[30]

DISUNITY CREATED BY POLITICS

The church has become as deeply divided along partisan political lines as our country has. Christians on the right and the left, those who call themselves orthodox or progressive, conservative or liberal, Republican or Democrat, compete for the designation "Christian" to promote and legitimize their political positions.

Dr. Thomas Oden points us to a deep truth: unity in Christ will never proceed from agreement on the issues themselves.

Political strategies for government action on behalf of the poor continue to divide us and always will. The very premise that we are going to create unity in Christ by our agreement on the Kyoto treaty, or equal pay for equal work, or military strategy, has deeply divided the body of Christ in our time . . . Ethical conflicts do not unify Christian believers.[31]

Let's pause and reflect upon Oden's point. Our unity is in our common faith around our acceptance of the truth that we are "all one in Christ Jesus" (Gal. 3:28), and are called to one hope through "one Lord, one faith, one baptism—one God and Father of us all" (Eph. 4:5–6). Political and social concerns do not provide the cohesion that faith in Christ brings to the Church. We may differ on many political issues and endorse differing solutions for social ills—but we can agree that love of God and love of neighbor will compel us to act in the best interest of our neighbor.

Sometimes we are divided by larger moral principles, such as the debate between what some call the culture of life vs. the culture of death. But most often we confuse Christian principles with whatever issues dominate the culture at any given time. As we attempt to make our faith relevant and attractive to our culture, we may find ourselves accommodating cultural and political influences that are detrimental to the church. The church aligns itself with political policies, whether they be pro-American policies or the policies of the United Nations or other ideological commitments.

On the other hand, there are times when these debates are over the best way to bring larger moral principles to bear. But even if our concepts of social justice were free of partisan political commitments, people will differ on how we achieve the goals of social justice. They will differ on how best to deliver social security for the least and marginalized in society, how to most effectively provide health care, and how racial reconciliation is to be promoted. Questions of appropriateness or desired outcome are often at the heart of debate over which policy best achieves the objective. The church is not the best vehicle to hammer out specific policies. Not only will someone have their political sensibilities offended, which contributes to disunity and decline, but the church is not equipped to make these types of policy decisions.

In our annual and general conferences we are often asked to endorse various legislative pieces without reliable or complete knowledge. Rarely are we presented with all the facts and considerations to be taken into account on any given issue. Even personnel in our boards and agencies often lack the expertise needed to weigh all the options on various legislative proposals before the church or society. We go beyond the expertise of our personnel and delegates when we ask them to interpret complicated economic and scientific data and theories.

When the church, in an official capacity, chooses sides in the honest debate about how to address social challenges and injustices, the social witness of the church can become a pawn for secular, and often partisan, agendas that seek legitimacy. Boards and agencies are given license to lobby for or against specific partisan proposals for which there is no denominational consensus or scriptural warrant. If we are locked into political commitments that we adhere to even when proven wrong by history or science, then we are blinded to "the way, the truth, and the life," which is the only true commitment that should engage us.

The primary focus of our social witness should not be on the political process. The state cannot solve all problems; the church should not think that it can.[32] That does not mean Christians should abandon the political process, but social witness is not about lobbying the faithful to take one political position over another. Why should the church pass judgment on every governmental policy decision, from political appointments to the theological certainty of tax policy and environmental policy, not to mention international commitments? George Weigel makes the point: "A partisan Gospel is an ideological Gospel, and as many of us insisted against the claims

> As we attempt to make our faith relevant and attractive to our culture, we may find ourselves accommodating cultural and political influences that are detrimental to the church.

of liberation theology in the 1970s and 1980s, an ideologically driven Gospel is a debasement of the Gospel."[33]

Mike McCurry, the former press secretary in the Clinton administration, was a delegate to the 2004 General Conference. He addressed a luncheon held by the Methodist Federation for Social Action. He lamented the polarizing effects of political commitments. He also advised that the church did not need to legislate on everything and "sometimes the best thing for our church is to sit and be quiet."[34]

Some suggest that those who disagree with their political position on poverty don't care about the less fortunate. This charge of apathy, or hostility, is raised whether the issue is the poor, racial relations, immigration, the environment, or other issues. In most cases, this is simply untrue. It is grossly unfair to attribute an attitude of no concern for these issues to those who may differ on solutions.

There is sometimes the problem of inconsistency and even hypocrisy as we seek to implement social justice. It is common to see the mainline churches ignore failure, corruption and scandal on the part of individuals and institutions who share their ideologically driven notions of social justice. The church condemns violence or torture, but only of certain groups. Other groups get a pass because they are either deemed the more oppressed or the more worthy. Principle is lost by inconsistent application. It disturbs many that the persecution of Christians seems to attract less attention than that of non-Christians. These and other inconsistencies divide the body— and the church ceases to be truly prophetic in calling all to a higher standard of justice.

A HIGHER CALLING

Christians of all persuasions should be concerned about social and political issues and systems that impact the daily lives of individuals. The principles we bring to bear upon our social witness are found in Scripture. Christians must approach political engagement with humility and with earnest prayer for divine guidance and wisdom.

When Christians do justice, it speaks loudly about God. And it can show those who are not believers how the Christian vision can contribute to the common good and help alleviate the ills of society. . . . As Christians committed to the full authority of Scripture, our normative vision must flow from the Bible and from the moral order that God has embedded in his creation. . . . Because social systems are complex and our knowledge is incomplete, we cannot predict all the effects of laws, policies, and regulations. As a result, we must match our high ideals with careful social analysis and critical reflection on our experience in order to avoid supporting policies that produce unintended and unfortunate consequences. . . . When we as Christians engage in political activity, we must maintain our integrity and keep our biblical values intact.[35]

The church has the incredible capacity of bringing a powerful witness to bear upon the culture and upon man-made political and social structures. The church embodies the principles of God, the creator and architect of all human experience. Let us not allow the church's witness to be drawn into compromise with prevailing social constructs where everyone and everything suffers.

Chapter Six
The Fallout of Church Failure

Pip: Methodists suffered a backlash from the Church of England, even though they fully participated in public worship and the sacraments of the Church of England. What guided you as you continued preaching and ministering beyond the established Church?

Wesley: It was clear to me, and those who worked alongside me, that God's will took priority over the opinions and organizations of men. We were of the opinion that we will obey the rules and governors of the Church whenever we can, consistently with our duty of God. Whenever we cannot, we will quietly obey God rather then men.[1] The greatest failure of a compromised Church is its failure to see souls saved and brought into a life of holiness. I expressed this to some degree in 1788 as I spoke of the necessity of moving beyond some of the points of discipline of the official Church. We did none of these things till we were convinced we could no longer omit them but at the peril of our souls.[2] When the Church fails to save souls, other failures will follow.

THE CONCERNS OF THE FAITHFUL
The Church of England and Methodist Rift

> Wesley was first, last, and always a churchman in the finest sense of the term. He lived and died a clergyman in the Church of England. He believed that authentic Christian experience had to be nurtured in community.[3]

John Wesley never intended to break with the Church of England. Yet, the Methodist movement he started with his brother became a separate denomination out of necessity. And despite the growth of Methodism and its far-reaching effect upon the English culture, the Church of England never reached out to embrace this movement. This is even more surprising given the fact that John Wesley insisted that Methodist converts attend worship and receive the sacraments through the national church, thereby swelling the ranks of the Church of England. One historian noted:

> No organic link existed at any time between the National Church and the United Societies of "the people called Methodist." . . . At no time did Anglican authorities . . . initiate means for the spiritual nurture of the rapidly multiplying Methodist Societies. . . . Considered in retrospect, it is astonishing that this nation-wide revival of spiritual religion, extending throughout half a century under the preaching and teaching of the Wesleys, and a few brother-clergy, evoked no immense body of converts organically within the ministrations of the Anglican Church.[4]

When the Church has lost its zeal and faithful commitment to the teachings of Scripture and to its own doctrinal standards, the tendency of an unfaithful leadership is to distance itself from, or attack, that which calls it to account. It is in such times that God raises up individuals, renewal groups, and parachurch organizations for the maintaining of an authentic Christian witness. John Wesley experienced strong opposition to his ministry. As Methodists today, we revere him and may not appreciate how he was scorned and even hated by his contemporaries. One such critic, John Kirkby, Church of England rector of Blackmanstoke, wrote in 1750 about "the horrid blasphemies and impieties taught by those diabolical seducers called Methodists."[5] Methodism was actually a renewal movement within the Church of England. Wesley's disagreements with the Church of England were not institutional, they were scriptural.[6]

Wesley saw the failure of the church to meet the spiritual needs of people. In regard to the Christianity of his day, Wesley asked:

> Why has Christianity done so little good in the world? Is it not the balm which the great Physician has given to men, to restore their spiritual health? . . . I am bold to affirm, that those who bear the name of Christ are in general totally ignorant, both to the theory and practice of Christianity; so that they are "perishing by thousands" for lack of knowledge and experience . . . of justification by faith, the new birth, inward and outward holiness. . . .[7]

Wesley abhorred stagnant orthodoxy and sought a scriptural Christianity energized by the ongoing presence of the Holy Spirit.[8] He was willing to pay the price of ostracism in order to faithfully proclaim this kind of scriptural Christianity.

Internal United Methodist Concerns

In his 1995 book, *Awakening from Doctrinal Amnesia*, Dr. William Abraham identified ten sources of anxiety for many United Methodist Church members. Abraham says many members are concerned about:

1. Declining membership;
2. Apportionments or monies sent to the central bureaucracies;
3. Alienation of many in the church from the central agencies of the church;
4. Current church leadership;
5. Seminaries;
6. Moral and doctrinal hollowness of the church in its preaching and teaching;
7. Encroachment of a radical agenda into the institutions and fabric of the church;

8. Institutional division within United Methodism;
9. The church's mission; and
10. That the church has lost its way spiritually.[9]

Based on these points, it's clear United Methodist members' differences with the church, unlike John Wesley's, are not only scriptural, but institutional as well. Because we are a reform movement gone off course, in proclaiming the Gospel and our social witness, we have far more to consider as we endeavor to reclaim our Wesleyan distinctives.

When the church fails, it fails not only its own membership, but the culture in which it is called to bear witness. The reformation Wesley brought in his day impacted those who accepted Christ as Lord and Savior—and, it also impacted the culture to which they returned as transformed people.

The inspiration, motivation, and foundation of Wesley's social witness was love, and the results were remarkable. Hearts were turned to God, a religious awakening commenced, many people rose out of economic want, and unjust laws and practices were addressed.

But something goes amiss when the by-products of faith—social programs or liberation of the oppressed—become the foundation of our witness.

The breakdown in the mission and ministry of the church today has led to loss of members, disunity, a confusion of purpose, and questions of credibility. But the church itself is not the only one to be weakened when the witness of the church embraces partisan ideology.

When the church fails, it fails not only its own membership, but the culture in which it is called to bear witness.

The Breakdown Within Society

Over the last fifty years, we have seen a major breakdown in American society at large. We can compare it to the breakdown in society in John Wesley's time.

The eighteenth century was marked by tumultuous social, economic, and spiritual upheaval. In the course of his life, Wesley witnessed the development of the industrial revolution which ushered England out of the Middle Ages into the modern era, resulting in the migration and displacement of millions of workers into the major cities. He also witnessed the dangerous polarization of economic classes and the insecurity experienced by the masses, who took retreat from the harshness of life in alcohol, violence, prostitution, and gambling. And sadly, Wesley witnessed the growing irrelevance of the Church of England in addressing these problems.

Let's consider some of the cultural challenges we face in the twenty-first century. Our time is different from Wesley's—yet not so different. Polarization and insecurity drive many today to seek relief in alcohol, drugs, and sex—or in wealth, power, and control.

The Reality for Women

The women's movement in the nineteenth century sought the right to vote, championed other women's rights, and provided leadership and momentum for the temperance movement. The twentieth century saw advances for women in many areas of their lives. In *Gaining Ground: A Profile of American Women in the Twentieth Century*, author Janice Crouse cites various United States governmental statistics to document the real strides made by and for women. Advances in medicine brought down death rates and increased life span. Women made outstanding educational gains, moving from 23 percent with a high school degree in 1940 to nearly 83 percent by 1998. By the end of the century, women had moved ahead of men in numbers of bachelor's and master's degrees earned. Many women pursued doctoral degrees and earned over 40 percent of all medical and law degrees.[10] By the first decade of the twenty-first century, there were more women than men pursuing medical and law degrees.

Women entered the labor force in record numbers during the last half of the twentieth century. The National Center for Policy Analysis notes that the single most important change in American society in the past sixty years has been the entry of women into the labor market. The number of women in the labor force more than doubled between 1950 and 2000, and women with children went from 12 percent of working women to more than 60 percent. They further note that "new Internal Revenue Service data confirm the growing equality of the sexes in terms of income." They indicate that many women now earn more than their male counterparts. Often statistics which show inequality are a result of women voluntarily moving in and out of the work force to care for children and the elderly.[11]

We should also be reminded that women have made strides within the church. In 2006, The United Methodist Church commemorated fifty years of women's ordination. More women are entering the ministry than ever before.

While celebrating these accomplishments for women, we do not ignore other areas where modernity has been especially detrimental to women. The cultural revolution begun in the '60s, which included the sexual liberation brought on by the development of the birth control pill, took its toll on women, children, youth, and men. Nowhere is this more evident than the breakdown of the family. Integral to understanding the breakdown is acknowledging the lack of commitment which has led to a rising divorce rate as well as out-of-wedlock births.

With the incredible strides women have made, feminists continue to see the status of women through the lens of oppression. The feminist movement of the 1960s was called the women's liberation movement. Women were thought to need liberating from marriage, moral standards, the raising of children, and patriarchal systems.

Feminists thought that the availability of contraception would bring down the rate of out-of-wedlock births. But that prediction did not turn out to be true. Even after abortion was made legal, the rate continued to rise. From 1965 to 1990, out-of-wedlock births jumped from 24 to 64 percent among African American women and from 3 to 18 percent among whites.

In an essay titled "Regarding Daughters and Sisters: The Rape of Dinah," Leon Kass notes:

> The sexual revolution, made possible by the contraceptive separation of sexual activity from its implicit generative consequences, deliberately sacrificed female virtue on the altar of the god of pleasure now. Not surprisingly, the result was emancipated male predation and exploitation, as men were permitted easy conquests of women without responsibility or lasting intimacy . . . the liberated women's movement mounted a moralistic political campaign against the "patriarchy," seeking power and respect, mistakenly believing that the respect women need as women is based solely on power.[12]

The moral laxity brought on by this agenda was particularly hard on the poor, and most detrimental to the inner city poor, who were often racial minorities. According to Crouse, there were "50 million unmarried women at the end of the twentieth century. Of the total number . . . more than one out of five lived in poverty and of those with school-age children under eighteen, more than one-third lived in poverty." This is tragic and stunning when compared to married-couple families, where one out of twenty lived below the poverty level.[13] Clearly the cultural revolution took a costly toll on the poor, and contributed to many women and children entering their ranks.

The Reality for Men

In an article titled "Men Without Children" which appeared in the *Economic Journal* in 1998, George Akerlof argued that one social consequence of the cultural revolution was the disappearance of marriage because men were allowed to avoid marriage even when they had fathered a child. Between 1968 and 1993, men aged 25–34 who were married with children fell from 66 to 40 percent. Akerlof noted that substance abuse and incarceration of young men doubled during this same time. He correlated the rise in substance abuse and incarceration to the growth of single men who were avoiding marriage.[14]

Other studies found that boys raised outside an intact nuclear family were twice as likely to end up in prison. In their book, *Growing*

Up with a Single Parent, Sarah McLanahan and Gary Sandefur not only documented this, but also reported research that showed children from divorced families are more likely to drop out of high school, and girls are more likely to have out-of-wedlock children.[15] Most disturbing was data that confirmed the avoidance of marriage and the prevalence of divorce and nonmarital birth had detrimental consequences which fell disproportionately on the shoulders of the poor.[16]

The Church's Failed Witness

Where was the church during this time? Many women of faith, influenced by theologies of liberation, adopted the themes of radical feminists. Birth control and abortion were seen as tools to free women from the consequences of the natural function of their bodies, which, according to this way of thinking, was oppressive when it led to unwanted pregnancy. Various feminist theologies emerged based on oppression in general and oppression of women specifically. Freedom from oppression came to include the freedom from being judged for what once had been considered immoral. The church failed to teach a thorough doctrine of sin and accommodated itself tragically to an increasingly secular society. As Martin Luther King Jr. said, "The church was merely a thermometer, when it should have been a thermostat, determining the moral and spiritual temperature of society, not just reflecting it."

In recent years, the right to abortion has been one of the key issues that some agencies of the church have championed. Shortly after *Roe v. Wade* became law in 1973, the Board of Church and Society and the Women's Division helped to form and became early members of the Religious Coalition for Abortion Rights (RCAR), an organization that lobbied Congress on abortion issues. It later changed its name to the Religious Coalition for Reproductive Choice (RCRC) in an effort to be less controversial. RCRC has generously funded, encouraged, and partnered with many organizations that promote unrestricted abortion and partial-birth abortion, both of which are contrary to The United Methodist Church's position in *The Book of Discipline.*

Unfortunately, other ways of tackling the problem of unwanted pregnancy go virtually neglected. There are no programs for establishing adoption agencies or homes for unwed mothers, aside from maintaining those United Methodist agencies that were established decades ago. Nor does the church advocate partnering with agencies outside the denomination that are currently actively addressing unwanted pregnancy from a pro-life position.

Programs that would call men and women to respect their bodies and God's standard for sexuality in the sacred bonds of marriage go undeveloped. Instead of coming alongside the family to prepare young men and women for the responsibility of life and love, the church has joined society at large in seeing traditional abstinence as an outdated ethic from which women have been liberated.

The Reality for the Family

The right of children to grow up in an intact, two-biological-parent family is rarely considered a matter of justice by the church. The authors of *Growing Up with a Single Parent* pointed out that an intact, two-parent family does four key things for children. Two parents bring economic resources and also model appropriate male-female relations, including virtues like fidelity and self-sacrifice in the context of a marital relationship. When both parents are invested in the child, they monitor one another's parenting, which reduces stress and forestalls abuse. Finally, fathers often serve as key guides to children seeking to negotiate the outside world.[17] After twenty years of research on the effects of family structure on children, they concluded that the best design for making sure that children's basic needs were met was something quite similar to the two-parent ideal.[18]

Has the church really neglected the care and nurture of this basic institution? Statistics confirm that among Christians, the rates of divorce, out-of-wedlock births, and abortion mirror that of society at large.[19] In our efforts to advocate for those in situations which are less than the Christian ideal, have we somehow failed the very family structure that is the basic building block of all just societies? It is the intact family that best provides for the nurture and education of the young to become mature responsible adults, capable of contributing to society. It is God's original design. In the words of W. Bradford Wilcox, "We must make it clear that the church's commitment to the poor requires nothing less than a vigorous proclamation of the church's true and beautiful teaching about sex and marriage . . . the preferential option for the poor begins in the home."[20]

In *How Now Shall We Live?*, Chuck Colson writes:

> When family breakdown becomes widespread, entire neighborhoods decay. Neighborhoods without fathers are often infected with crime and delinquency. They are often places where teachers cannot teach because misbehaving children disrupt classrooms. Moreover, children of divorce are much more likely to get divorced themselves as adults, so that the negative consequences pass on to the next generation. In this way, family breakdown affects the entire society.[21]

As long as we see the problem in terms of rights to be fought for and liberation to be won, we fail to do the serious deep theological work that would mitigate the consequences of the Fall that affect both men and women. We fail to truly understand and appreciate that we were created in God's image; male and female (Gen. 2:27). We need to recover a deeper understanding of our need for one another in community. Instead of seeing ourselves in competition, the church should help men and women rediscover how we complement and complete each other. In part, this means understanding a child's need of both a father and a mother and their distinct roles. A rejection of liberation theologies as they apply to sex and marriage will go a long way in healing the sexual confusion and brokenness that prevails within our society.

Certainly, the church must reach out to all with the love of Christ. Stigmatizing and shaming those who fall short is wrong. The church has reached out to single women, the divorced, single parents, women facing unwanted pregnancy, and those living in alternative lifestyles. This is good. What we must commit to is the family which is built on Jesus' definition of marriage—one man and one woman joined together by God in one flesh (Mark 10:6–9). Our neglect has fueled the brokenness that is the natural outcome of traditional family breakdown. Promoting righteousness (right living, God's way) is, and has always been, in the public interest of all societies.

The Church and "Rights"

This will mean that some of our political commitments need to be rethought. Instead of passing resolutions calling The United Methodist Church to ratify the controversial United Nations Treaty on the Rights of the Child, for example, we should be working to secure the opportunity for every child to grow up in an intact family. Today, even in the church, we seem to find it difficult to talk about what is "right" or "moral." We have championed the rights of those who have not had the benefit of intact family structures, yet we seem unable to champion the family structure that would help alleviate many of the problems that stem from broken families.

> Promoting righteousness (right living, God's way) is, and has always been, in the public interest of all societies.

One aspect of the social witness of the church that should be rethought is the tendency to advocate serious social issues exclusively in terms of "rights." God has created all people in His image with certain rights. When basic rights are neglected or abused, it is important for the church to call society to task. This is an important part of the social dimension of Wesley's own work for the poor, the incarcerated, even the uneducated. In more recent times, the drafting of the United Nations International Declaration of Humans Rights in 1948 is laudable, as is the work of the civil rights movement in this country. We should remember, however, that "rights," in and of themselves, take society only so far in the quest for justice.

Today, all too often "wants" are confused with "rights" in serious issues such as the right to die or the right to same-sex marriage. In such cases, advocating for something in the name of rights preempts all reasoned discussion. Individuals and societies may desire to do wrong and advocate the right to do wrong. The church must teach what is right as set forth in God's revealed word. A right is not the same thing as what is right.[22] God created us to have free will. We may choose to do what is wrong or what is right. But, all through the Old and New Testaments, God makes it clear what the consequences of our choices will ultimately be. To be just and fair, the Church must be clear and faithful to teach this reality as it has been put forth in Scripture. It is profoundly unjust to teach or advocate for a partial truth.

THE WESLEYAN MODEL

Much of the societal breakdown we see today can be understood, in part, due to the severing of rights from responsibility. John Wesley was successful because his social advocacy was rooted in a love for the individual. He understood that one's well-being would come not only by securing rights, but also by fostering responsibility—both personal and social. Consider the issue of alcoholism. During Wesley's time, there was widespread consumption of alcohol, "the extent of which is hardly imaginable even in our own time."[23] It's hard to imagine Wesley arguing that the poor had a right or even an excuse for drunkenness. He did call attention to the use of grain in the alcohol industry which contributed to scarcity and high prices, in turn leading to hunger. But he also addressed temperance as an issue of holiness, believing "alcohol abuse would gradually destroy the body and soul."[24]

Wesley urged all people, regardless of their economic standing, to deal with sin and habits that contributed to their misfortune and that of others. He encouraged discipline and developing habits and virtues that benefited both the individual and community. Wesley was convinced that following scriptural principles, thriftiness, personal denial, and stewardship would naturally lead to greater financial standing. Above all, he encouraged all to see themselves as beloved sons and daughters of their heavenly Father. When individuals embraced who they were in Christ, they grew in Christ-likeness and inevitably improved their life.

Wesley called the rich to visit the poor and become personally involved in helping them. Those of means were called to their responsibility to love their neighbor and provide for their needs. Giving of money and resources was important, but duty did not stop there for Wesley. He did not exempt any rung on the economic ladder from responsibility.

The "Victimization" Problem

Wesley realized that the poor were victims of some conditions over which they had no control, but he did not excuse them from dealing with sin and growing in righteousness. He believed people should take responsibility for their situations, rather than blaming circumstances, family, environment, fate, or anything else. For Christians, this is possible because of personal redemption and the power of the indwelling Holy Spirit. How different this is today! Much has been written about the victim mentality pervasive in today's culture. A disturbing consequence is the belief that we cannot be held responsible for our bad choices or actions, since they are caused by what others have done to us or what "the system" has done to us.

Obviously, in many instances, there are extenuating circumstances, but most thoughtful Americans believe that we have gone too far in providing people with excuses. The challenge for those who advocate for the poor or oppressed is to offer more than political remedies. We need to recover the biblical teachings which lead to abundant life.

Today's church could go a long way toward improving lives if it were to seriously teach and call all to a deeper sense of personal responsibility. Young people and adults in all walks of life have failed to take advantage of opportunities available in our society; many fall victim to drugs, sex, alcohol, or just fail to mature as they move into adulthood. Philip Johnson said:

> Instead of talking about "who gets what," we need to talk about "who contributes what" . . . Ordinary people who raise their children to put in more than they take out. . . . These are the kinds of people who supply the moral capital that makes social justice achievable.[25]

John Wesley was successful because his social advocacy was rooted in a love for the individual.

Johnson wanted to see society stop undermining the values that make people responsible citizens and start reinforcing them. What better place for this to begin than in the church?

The church must uphold the truth it has been given—there is grace unleashed by the life, death, and resurrection of Christ that can liberate people from bondage to sin, addictions, and an unending cycle of irresponsible behavior. This is a reality. The government does not have the resources to change or alter this cycle of self-destruction, and throwing money and programs at the problem cannot break this cycle . . . only the grace of God in Jesus Christ can. The Church is God's messenger through which truth is offered to society.

AN ETERNAL LOSS

Not long ago, a United Methodist woman wrote to a renewal group expressing her deep concern about the divisions within The United Methodist Church. She identified some of the key problems, as she saw them, and concluded with the statement, "We are maintaining the status quo, while souls, souls, precious souls are perishing." Her sentiments would seem to be those of John Wesley himself.

The salvation of individuals through faith in Jesus Christ was Wesley's first priority. But that was not the end of it. Dr. H. T. Maclin, former GBGM missionary and president of The Mission Society, spoke of the next steps in his paper, "The World Is Our Parish." Those who have responded to the invitation of salvation next hear Jesus ask them to become his disciples. "The way Jesus put it to them, becoming a disciple was costly . . . ."[26]

Maclin says that before God asks us to *go*, he asks us to *come*, then to *follow*. Unfortunately, through many of our denominational programs and literature, and within many of our churches, we ask people to go, often into political and social activism, without inviting them to saving faith and committed discipleship at a personal level. We have seen some progress in this area through the Walk to Emmaus program, through Disciple Bible Study, and more recently through Christian Believer. Proclaiming the Gospel is not a priority, however, in many of our church-related program resources. The social and political priority of our boards and agencies is reflected in the resolutions they promote.

The result: "Souls, souls, precious souls are lost."

Chapter Seven
When the Gospel Is Preached and Holiness Pursued

Pip: You preached often from Matthew 7:21–27, the portion of Jesus' Sermon on the Mount that references building on sand or rock. How can we be sure that we are building on the rock?

Wesley: Wise, therefore, are those who build on Christ and establish him as their only foundation. They trust only in His blood and righteousness and in what He has done and suffered for us all. Wise persons fix their faith on this cornerstone and rest the entire weight of their souls upon it.[1] Renounce all hope of ever being able to save yourself. Place all your hope on being washed in Christ's blood and cleansed by His Spirit. Let nothing satisfy you other than the power of godliness—a religion that is spirit and life. . . . Be amazed and humbled to the dust by the love of God in Christ Jesus. . . . Be a person who loves God and all humankind. In this spirit, do and endure everything. Demonstrate your faith by your works, and in this way you will do the will of your Father in heaven. As you now walk with God on earth, you will also reign with Him in glory.[2]

BUILDING ON THE ROCK

Social Justice Surprises

The Church has shown the compassionate heart of Jesus Christ to a fallen, hurting world. Christians of all theological, political, and social persuasions have heard the call to care for "the least of these." Nonetheless, there are some social justice surprises when data is examined.

What about the effectiveness of today's social programs that clearly emphasize the sharing of the Gospel of Christ? Teen Challenge is a program, begun by the Rev. David Wilkerson in 1958. This ministry for teens and adults with addictions continues today with 170 centers in the United States. Teen Challenge has one of the highest freedom-from-addiction success rates of similar organizations. A study of program graduates done at Teen Challenge of Chattanooga, Tennessee, in 1994 showed:

- 67 percent were abstaining from illegal drugs and alcohol;
- 76 percent of the respondents attended church regularly;
- 92 percent said that Teen Challenge had been a great impact on their lives;
- 80 percent credited developing a personal relationship with Jesus Christ as a major influence in helping them stay off drugs.

In fact, the study credited the success of the Teen Challenge program to its emphasis on a vibrant faith in Jesus Christ.[3]

Stephen V. Monsma, formerly a political scientist at Pepperdine University, then a research fellow at the Paul B. Henry Institute for the Study of Christianity and Politics at Calvin College, conducted a four-year study of five hundred welfare-to-work programs in Chicago, Los Angeles, Philadelphia, and Dallas. He discovered there were more evangelical programs than mainline Protestant programs. Perhaps this is because the mainlines tend to concentrate much of their effort on lobbying Congress for expanded government-run welfare programs. He also found that clients of evangelical programs more often referenced the caring nature of the staff, despite the fact they also showed that caring with "tough love."

Monsma concluded, "Evangelical programs can compete with anyone else in terms of effectiveness."[4]

Long-range effectiveness is certainly a hallmark of the Christian Community Development Association (CCDA), a successful ministry committed to building the community and the family among the poor. Begun by John Perkins in the 1960s, this multiracial, inner-city ministry offers Christ and offers help. Over the years Perkins has hammered out the "Three R's of Development"— reconciliation, relocation, and redistribution.

Reconciliation shows itself as a multiracial ministry. Relocation emphasizes that to work with the poor you have to live with them. Redistribution may sound like socialism, but Perkins seeks economic vitality, not handouts, emphasizing the need for opportunity and the self-confidence to take advantage of opportunity. Perkins says, "What we wanted CCDA to be is first of all Christian, believing the Bible is the Word of God, but also practical for living."[5] This combination of being a Bible-believing Christian who reaches out to touch lives in practical and ministering ways comes from a compassionate heart.

Who Really Cares?

In *Who Really Cares*, Arthur C. Brooks, a preeminent public policy expert who spent years researching giving trends in America, was surprised by what he found.

He identified four forces in modern American life that are primarily responsible for making people charitable: religion, skepticism about the government in economic life, strong families, and personal entrepreneurialism. These forces go a long way in addressing our social problems. He clarified that government spending is not charity because it is not a voluntary sacrifice by individuals. Below are a few of the interesting facts disclosed in Brooks' research:

■ Religious people are inarguably more charitable in every measurable way. Religious people are far more charitable than nonreligious people. "In years of research," reports Brooks, "I have never found a measurable way in which secularists are more charitable than religious people."

- Welfare supporters give less than welfare opponents—and welfare recipients give less than non-welfare recipients who are equally poor.
- People who favor government income redistribution are significantly less likely to behave charitably than those who do not.
- Conservative families gave more than liberal families within every income class. Strong intact religious families also passed on the virtue of generosity to their children.
- Young liberals—perhaps the most vocally dissatisfied political constituency in America today—are one of the least generous demographic groups.

Brooks found, again to his own surprise, that conservative and religious people also volunteer more of their time to charitable causes than their liberal counterparts.[6] He wrote:

When I started doing research on charity, I expected to find that political liberals—who, I believed genuinely cared more about others than conservatives did—would turn out to be the most privately charitable people. So when my findings led to the opposite conclusion, I assumed I had made some sort of technical error. I re-ran analyses. I got new data. Nothing worked. In the end, I had no option but to change my views. I confess the prejudices of my past here to emphasize that the findings in this book—many of which may appear conservative and support a religious, hardworking, family-oriented lifestyle—are faithful to the best available evidence, and contrary to my political and cultural roots.[7]

While not all religious or evangelical persons would consider themselves to be conservative, these findings are helpful to our focus. They point back to our early Methodist roots when the Gospel and social witness bore no antipathy toward each other, but rather, works followed righteousness.

The records of giving and service in The United Methodist Church tend to confirm Brooks's research. The majority of our largest churches and our largest membership per capita are found in the Southeastern Jurisdiction and in the North and South Central

Jurisdictions. These are the areas that pay the largest apportionments and have proportionately more second-mile giving. By contrast, in our more liberal conferences across the nation, there are more church closings due to dwindling congregations.

We should keep in mind that Brooks's work deals in generalizations. Nevertheless, in the debate over the social witness of the church and how issues of justice are to be addressed, it is not a matter of changing the social witness from a liberal platform to a conservative one. It is about faithfulness to the mission of the church.

By putting aside the stereotypical myths that conservatives are unloving and nongiving, we can move on to examine some examples within The United Methodist Church of individuals and churches faithfully proclaiming the Gospel of Jesus Christ and bearing a strong social witness. This is truly the Wesleyan way.

SOME STERLING EXAMPLES

A Family's Service in Offering Christ

The family reported here is real, but they asked that their name and location not be used.

Twenty-five years ago, a family we'll call the Georges was asked to host a male youth during the Thanksgiving holiday. The others at his group home were all returning to their families, but he was not allowed to because of problems within the biological family. The wife and husband agreed to help because, as they said, "they had some space."

When Christmas came, the same young man was in need. Again the couple agreed. After Christmas, the Georges and the young man's social worker discussed the long-term needs of the youth. The couple agreed to let him live with them, but set some conditions on the arrangement. The young man:

- Must participate in church;
- Must do the same level of chores as others in the home;
- Must do all his school work; and
- Must not pose any threat to the couple's two preschool children.

In exchange, the Georges agreed to:

- Help the young man gain basic daily living skills and interpersonal skills for future employment;
- Assist every night with homework;
- Provide basic guidance in Christianity—though without compulsion beyond the expectation that the young man would participate in church activities with the family; and
- Treat the young man like biological family.

The young man eventually graduated from high school, though he did have some brushes with the law. He entered full-time employment thanks to help from one of his biological brothers in another state.

Taking in people was not new to this couple. They had previously hosted an international student each summer while she attended college in the U.S. This pattern continued until it became simply a holy habit for the couple and, then, their children.

Over the years, the Georges took in various people, including several desperately poor boys whose mother was raising them in a home without plumbing and with only bare bulbs for light. This mother ceded parental authority so the young men could be covered by the Georges' insurance and to permit the couple to interact with the schools. The boys shared a bedroom with the couple's son and he served as a big brother; the couple's daughter was like a big sister. The son helped the boys with sports, and the daughter tutored them in math. As with the first foster son, the family and the boys agreed to mutual care and respect. These two young men returned to their home state but later both went to prison. They maintained communication with the family, though, and now both have come to Christ and are attempting to reorder their lives in spite of their difficulties.

More recently, the Georges have taken in students whose parents left the state for employment elsewhere. The students wanted to finish school in the town where they had lived for years. In addition, several college and graduate students who needed assistance or simply convenient housing stayed with this family.

Mr. George was asked whether all the effort was worth it. He said:

It wasn't that much effort. People stay with us. They eat what they want, but clean up after themselves. They have to seek to improve themselves and, yes, some of them have really come from terribly bad situations with a lot weighing them down. In spite of jail time and difficulty finding employment for some, all have improved their lot and all have seen the Gospel lived in at least some feeble way. What would be the point of only taking in people who had no problems? We genuinely believe that this is a means of God's grace for us. We gain more than they, so offering hospitality to those who for a brief time may have a need is a blessing— sometimes an inconvenient blessing, certainly one that costs us money—but a blessing, truly, a blessing nonetheless. You know, we do this as family, but I know others who do it, too—very incon- spicuous hospitality. And, then, there are others who really do a lot, like the Good Works people over in southeast Ohio—now, that's real service in the Name of Jesus Christ.

Perhaps most telling was what their now-adult daughter said:

I was having a conversation with one of my peers at work the other day and I mentioned one of the young men who currently was staying in my parents' home. This person asked who they were and I explained. My friend seemed taken aback, almost startled. You know, I was equally surprised, because I realized for the first time that this was not the typical. And, I thought to myself, "It should be." I guess if your moral inertia propels you to kindness it's simply easier to be kind than not. If you have a habit of helping it is just less trouble to help than not to.

Her father smiled and said, "There you go. This has been as much or more for our biological children and ourselves as the way grace works in our lives as for any of those we've had stay with us."

Camp Paraguay: A Ministry to the *Mestizos* of Paraguay

If John Wesley were alive today, would he be interested in Paraguay? The answer is so obvious. Wesley called for Methodists to be very intentional and methodical in their faith and discipleship. Few will argue against the understanding that our mission as United Methodist Christians is to make disciples of Jesus Christ internationally. Today, the Wesleyan motto, "The world is my parish," rings in our ears continuously.

According to Wesley, God desires to renew us in the love of Christ, to restore us to the full image of God and to make a new creation in Christ. Wesley believed that God's new creation applies not only to us as individuals but also to the culture in which we live. This is in tune with what the Lord commands us to pray: "Thy Kingdom come, thy will be done, on earth as it is in heaven."

Indeed, John Wesley expected that the spiritual transformation of the heart would affect the entire society and the world. In the eighteenth century, Wesley did not use the words "healing of the broken world" as we use it today. His concept of spiritual transformation, however, clearly envisioned this healing of brokenness. Wesley said the grace of God is the "therapeutic power of God."[8]

Paraguay is not an easy field in which to plant Methodism. Those trying to plant a Protestant church in Paraguay face enormous resistance. Roman Catholicism is the official religion and thus anti-Protestant sentiment is strong. Protestant mission is sometimes considered a cult, so most people do not want to have anything to do with it.[9]

Methodist work in Paraguay began under the auspices of The Mission Society for United Methodists in 1983. No significant fruits were reaped until two Brazilians, the Rev. Norival Trindada and his wife, Ruth, assisted by the Rev. Pablo Mora and his wife, Claudette, along with a handful of Brazilian missionaries, put their hands on this spiritually barren land.

The Rev. Chul Ki Kim, a Methodist missionary from the Korean Methodist church, planted a church among Korean immigrants in Paraguay. Mora and Kim collaborated to found the Evangelical Methodist Community of Paraguay in Asunción, the capital of

Paraguay. In 2007, the construction of Paraguayan Evangelical Methodist Seminary will be completed. These efforts continue to bear fruit, but there is much left for Methodists to do in Paraguay.

In 2003, the Rev. Kenny Yi, senior pastor of New York Plainview United Methodist Church, was invited by the Korean Methodist Church in Paraguay to hold a revival for the Korean immigrants in Paraguay. While he stayed at a hotel in Asunción, the vision of the healing of brokenness for a particular group was conceived.

It all started with a simple TV program. Yi turned on the TV in his hotel room. It was just an evening show, a Paraguayan program similar to CBS's *60 Minutes*. He casually watched a program presenting a Korean-Paraguayan girl, wearing typical Korean dress. She was crying before the camera and a *televista* (reporter) asked her why she was crying. She answered the *televista* that she cried because she didn't know where her Korean father was.

The next morning, Yi made contact with the Korean Embassy in Paraguay trying to obtain more detailed information about the Korean *mestizo* (half-Korean, half-Paraguayan) children. In Paraguay, it is estimated that there are more than a few thousand Para-Asian children living under the care of their mothers or grandmothers. Two-thirds of them are known to be Korean *mestizos*.

When the Overseas Emigration Law was passed in December 1962, Koreans began immigrating to South America. By official Korean statistics, it is estimated about 120,000 people entered South America between the years 1975–1990, but many more have gone undocumented. Most came looking for a new start and new financial opportunities.

Of those families that came to South America, many moved on to the United States and Canada. Some of those sojourning men

Indeed, John Wesley expected that the spiritual transformation of the heart would affect the entire society and the world.

started relationships with Paraguayan women. Some married and had families, while others were just looking for a good time. Many of these men moved on to other countries, leaving these women and children behind with no word as to where they were going or when they intended to return. The rate of abandoned children increased and now it is estimated that there are 2,000–3,000 *mestizos* in Paraguay.

After a series of attempts, Yi met a nine-year-old *mestizo* girl, Yijae (pronounced as "Jihey"). She had a beautiful smile and big, brown eyes, but she was quiet and kept to herself. Something common, some kind of kinship made these two people able to relate to each other. They began with some small talk about her age and her family. She came with her grandmother and her two brothers.

When the conversation turned more personal, toward the question of who her parents were, her eyes were immediately wet and tears ran down her cheeks. She didn't know where her father was. Rev. Yi changed the conversation toward soccer and to other pleasures that nine-year-olds enjoy. Around them were the sounds of other kids like her. Yijae wasn't the only one who didn't know where her father was. They were all fatherless; all of their fathers were Korean immigrants.

Every one of these forgotten children is a precious treasure to God. They, too, are part of God's family and as believers we are called to be the first to reach out to orphaned children. Wesley's concept of divine grace, a therapeutic power of God, should be employed in the healing of these broken children—not only from physical separation from their earthly fathers, but also from spiritual separation from the heavenly Father.

God has always had a plan in place to protect and provide for these deserted children. His plan is and always has been that His followers would seek and serve those forgotten children. New York Plainview UMC immediately responded and organized a mission team to minister to the needs of those *mestizo* children in Paraguay.

The church sent its first short-term Volunteers In Mission (VIM) team to Paraguay in 2003, and they visited many of these children. These families were found in Korean churches, where their Paraguayan mothers or grandmothers continue to teach them about their culture and language. Many of these children were living in extreme poverty.

As a predominately Korean congregation, Plainview UMC members felt it was their responsibility to do something about this injustice. They used James 1:27 as their guide: "Religion that God our Father accepts as pure and faultless is this: to look after orphans and widows in their distress and to keep oneself from being polluted by the world." As Christians who believe that all human beings sin and need forgiveness from the Savior, they felt a call to care for these children on behalf of God, the great Father, and to ask these mothers and wives for forgiveness for the ways that their Korean fathers had sinned against them.

Camp Paraguay was started in 2003 to care for the needs of *mestizo* children. Certain requirements are necessary to be a part of the program. The ministry serves children who are in need of financial support so they can thrive in life and come to a saving knowledge of Jesus Christ.

Each month, families from the New York Plainview UMC sponsor children and pay for their tuition, food, and clothes. The family becomes spiritual parents to the children in Paraguay. They send letters and gifts as a means of encouraging and loving the child, and in the summer have the opportunity to meet the child through mission trips.

A youth team from Plainview goes to Paraguay to run a camp for the children. This provides a time to worship together, play games, and share stories and talents with each other. They have also created opportunities for these children to learn how to play musical instruments, to have Bible studies, and to receive pastoral care and counseling. This is a great time for mission volunteers to really love and care for these kids who have experienced so much hardship in their lives, and to show them that there is a God who is their Father and will love them and be their supporter and provider throughout their entire lives.

The ministry began with only a handful of kids. But through connections and word of mouth, more than sixty-five families have been discovered who need help and who are living in extreme poverty—and the numbers continue to grow.

Recently, Camp Paraguay extended its ministry. The camp opened a small vocational school for the mothers, teaching them sewing and hairdressing. They have also enabled the older teens to give back to their community by training them to become Bible study leaders for little children in the rural town of Falcon on the Paraguayan/Argentinian border. They acquired a deserted church and remodeled it so that older *mestizo* teens may have opportunities to serve the children in the rural town.

As these children grow up and mature into healthy men and women who love God, Plainview members are grateful for the blessing it has been to serve them. They hope and pray that this ministry will continue on in the hands of the children themselves and that they may become beacons of light in their country, sharing the love and grace of Jesus Christ with all.[10]

Answering the Call to Go and Make Disciples

From its earliest beginnings in 1822 as a mission to the Cherokee Indians, the congregation of the Guntersville First United Methodist Church in Guntersville, Alabama, has taken seriously the call in Matthew 28 to go and make disciples. Although faced with challenges along the way, Guntersville UMC has met them head on and continues to see its outreach expanded and strengthened.

The ministries of Guntersville UMC are built on a foundation of prayer. Each Sunday morning a team of committed prayer partners arrives at seven o'clock, stops in every room and by every pew, and lifts up those who will be attending and those who will be teaching. At 7:45 this team moves to the prayer chapel and lays hands on and prays with the pastor and church staff.

Vital to the life of the church is the P.A.C.E. Shepherding ministry, which ensures that each member is connected and cared for regularly. Shepherds are church members who have agreed to care for five church families with Prayer every day, with Availability when there is a need, with Contact every week, and with Example by exemplifying the love of Christ to their shepherd families.

Four worship services, each with a different style, provide an opportunity for spiritual growth. Whether it is a traditional or a contemporary setting, members may praise God in a way most meaningful to them.

Lay leadership and lay involvement are the keys to Guntersville UMC's strong support in local and global outreach. The community Thanksgiving meal was started by members and serves more than nine hundred people in Marshall County each year. Habitat for Humanity, Meals On Wheels, CASA, Hospice, The Kairos prison ministry, Emmaus, mission trips to Ecuador, and support of seven overseas missionary families provide the opportunity to give to others and to be ambassadors for Jesus Christ.

Three new outreach ministries have been added during the past year including GENESIS, which provides not only worship but programs to give people a hand up rather than a handout. The GENESIS worship service has been designed to reach those who would not enter a traditional church building. This is more than another contemporary service. GENESIS focuses on hard-core problems and needs that can only be helped by Jesus Christ. It is a service designed for the unsaved. Some of the programs offered at GENESIS include tutoring, parenting classes, financial planning, anger management, and Celebrate Recovery. GENESIS operates as a church—an extension of First United Methodist—offering help, with Jesus Christ at the center.

The second new ministry, So-Far, was started as an outreach to the residents of Cedar Lodge, a drug rehabilitation center. So-Far team members, who depend heavily on Guntersville First United Methodist Church Women and United Methodist Men, commit time every Saturday to give testimonies, lead worship, and share the grace and love of Jesus Christ with residents, helping them to understand that they are not alone and that help is available to them through Jesus. Numerous persons have invited Jesus into their hearts as a result of this ministry.

Stepping Ahead is a Christ-centered transitional facility designed to help people get their lives back together and find jobs after recovering from drug addiction. Started by Guntersville UMC member Dr. Mary Holley in conjunction with her nationally recognized MAMa (Mothers Against Methamphetamine), many from the church have joined her to help make Stepping Ahead a reality in Marshall County.

Another support group started by church members is SAFE, a ministry to abused women. Two brave women from the church stepped out and shared their testimonies with the congregation, and with much prayer SAFE was born and continues to be successful in helping women deal with hurts and trauma.

The VEIN Bunch was started by a husband and wife team who felt God calling them to begin a ministry to those recovering from or going through heart-related illnesses. Members of the VEIN Bunch are the first to arrive at the hospital when any church members are going through heart surgery. Strong support is offered in the recovery process.

With the exception of the GENESIS ministry, the outreach programs listed above were started by and continue to be administered by members of the church. Staff approval is necessary for a new ministry to begin, but once approved, the staff steps back, serving in a support capacity.

Guntersville UMC has not forgotten the youth and children, offering ministries to these groups that are exciting, active, and growing at a fast pace. Kids Korner, the church's daycare program has an enrollment of 133. In this program, children have the opportunity to learn about God five days a week. Sunday school, Kids On The Move, Church Alive, vacation Bible school, and family nights also provide children with excellent opportunities to learn about Jesus in a kid-friendly atmosphere.

Youth gather each week for UMYF, Sunday school, and boys' and girls' Bible studies, providing opportunities for fellowship, good fun, questions, and most of all, spiritual growth. Every year the youth participate in several off-campus activities such as Behold, winter retreat, and mission trips, along with local mission activities.

Numerous adult classes are offered through Sunday school, Church Alive, and weekday Bible studies for men and women in homes and at the church to help people grow in their love for Jesus Christ and then go and serve.

In 1987, the average worship attendance was 212; it has steadily increased to an average worship attendance of 633 in 2006. Many of those who have joined were not churchgoers but are now active members of our congregation who are reaching out to others.

Guntersville First United Methodist Church is made up of many individuals—some with a rich Christian heritage and others new in their walk with Christ—yet all are enriched, strengthened, and encouraged as they use the gifts God has given to help others and to share the Good News about our Lord and Savior, Jesus Christ.

A Rural Church Offering Christ

Mt. Zion UMC in Mercer County, Kentucky, is and, as far as anyone knows, has always been a strongly evangelical congregation. Membership has varied over the church's existence. The building sits across the Kentucky River from the site where Frances Asbury formed Bethel Academy, the first Methodist educational institution west of the Appalachians. It was built in 1839 and the sanctuary has never been significantly altered. Indeed, though there has been a small classroom addition, the building still does not include running water. The outhouse is about forty feet from the front door.

Eight years ago, the church was on the verge of closing. Though served by hard-working student pastors, the loss of farming population and the physical barrier of the Kentucky River that separated the church from the growth area of Kentucky's Bluegrass Region meant that the church did not have a natural constituency base. Still, the six regulars who attended each Sunday remained committed to allowing their church to serve as a field site for student learning.

Dr. James Thobaben, a professor of bioethics at Asbury Theological Seminary, had previously pastored in Appalachian Ohio and had founded a cooperative parish. He agreed to serve the church on two conditions: that the congregation continue to allow a high level of student participation; and that, except for preaching and administrative tasks for the annual conference, the students and community members would perform the congregational tasks.

After several years of ministry and growth, including the addition of a weekly prison ministry, Thobaben went on sabbatical. He asked Tapiwa Mucherera, professor of pastoral care at Asbury, to pastor the church for three weeks of each month. Thobaben would return on the fourth Sunday from the University of Missouri, where he was a visiting ethics scholar. After a year, they agreed to co-pastor.

The congregation grew to the building's capacity, with around ninety in attendance.

Building on the expectations established between Thobaben and the congregation and Mucherera's connections with communities in sub-Saharan Africa, the congregation decided to support orphanages serving children whose parents had died of AIDS.

Funds from Mt. Zion are used to buy diesel grinding mills and fuel for those mills. The orphanages, in turn, grind maize and indigenous grains for individuals in exchange for a percentage of the meal produced. This is the food for the orphanage; some is traded for other dietary necessities. Mt. Zion has paid for Mucherera and several parishioners to go to Zimbabwe to teach and to serve with Zimbabweans in helping these children. Currently, the church supplies enough resources to feed more than three thousand children daily.

Mucherera has moved to the other campus of Asbury Seminary, located in Florida. In his place, a lay employee of the seminary, Janelle Vernon, and a professor of Asbury College, Ken Pickerill, have agreed to help Thobaben and congregants continue the local and international ministries.

The congregation has fewer than twenty members and fewer than one hundred in weekly attendance. Yet, besides feeding these children every day, the congregation:

- offers the Gospel every Sunday night in a state prison;
- has funded short-term medical or educational missions to Haiti, the Dominican Republic, and Zimbabwe;
- sent service teams to assist with clean-up following Hurricane Katrina;
- adopted a highway for litter pick-up, and has also reached out to various local families;
- and is currently considering additional outreach to urban homeless in a nearby city.

What are the specific practices at Mt. Zion that make this outreach possible?

- Service and the core Gospel teaching of eternal salvation are strongly yoked through historical Wesleyan theology. The assumption is that one must accept forgiveness and justification by Jesus Christ and must then manifest that love in purity and service, not only for the sake of others but also as a means of grace for the individual to grow in holiness. In other words, the congregation "offers them Christ" in the full sense;

- The preaching frequently includes social justice and service as examples, with the assumption that personal purity and social care are simply different manifestations of behavior shaped by sanctifying grace;

- The pastors are actively involved in the church's work— they come to clean-up days, they go to the prison, they give their money;

- The expenditures for missions is more than 80 percent of the church budget. This is due in large part to the pastors being part-time;

- The congregation supports the ministries of the church with sacrificial giving. They embrace the idea that Christians serve, and that service is costly in time and money. No collection is taken during the service, but the collection plate is available at the back of the sanctuary after the service;

- The congregation decides how money will be spent. Mission expenditures are endorsed in congregational votes prior to the spending of the money. Since all the formal church members are on the administrative board, this satisfies any disciplinary requirement. For example, the congregation recently voted not to buy the house next door when it went up for sale. The building could have been used for local outreach and, certainly, having running water and a kitchen would prove advantageous on some occasions. Members concluded, however, that there was not enough money to buy the house and maintain it and to continue providing the same level of outreach;

- Members are encouraged to participate in Christ-centered small group ministries beyond those within the local church;

- Monthly activities and small groups intentionally include everyone who wants to participate;
- The non-clergy fully participate in church ministry, understanding that distinctions exist for gifts and skills but not status before our Lord. For instance, a local builder coordinates both the Katrina service and road pick-up because he has the equipment and the skills.

Perhaps the most interesting aspect of Mt. Zion's outreach is that it is considered unremarkable. Members don't boast about their service; rather, they believe they are simply doing what is expected of them as followers of Christ.

The congregation's standard (though each participant readily would admit that the standard has yet to be fully met), is found in Wesley's sermon "Of the Church":

> In the meantime, let all those who are real members of the Church see that they walk holy and unblameable in all things. . . . Show them your faith by your works. Let them see, by the whole tenor of your conversation, that your hope is laid up above! Let all your words and actions evidence the spirit whereby you are animated! Above all things, let your love abound; let it extend to every child of man; let it overflow to every child of God. By this let all men know whose disciples ye are, because you love one another.[11]

Other Examples

Kirbyjon Caldwell, senior pastor of Windsor Village UMC in Houston, Texas, writes:

> As it says in the book of Psalms, unless there is economic justice, there will be no peace in the community. Unless there is peace in the community, there will be no peace among individuals. If there's no peace among the individuals, then Satan has one more welcome mat to walk across.

But Caldwell is not talking about economic justice without proclamation of the Gospel—he's talking about economic justice as one part of that proclamation. "This is not a name-it, claim-it theology," he has said. It's a theology that begins at the Cross of Christ, with a relationship and repentance, and then causes transformation—both individually and socially—in every area of life.

The Power Center, which is operated by one of the four not-for-profit corporations Windsor Village has spawned to target community needs, has been called "the model for urban life" and "one of the best examples of community empowerment in Houston."

But Kirbyjon Caldwell just calls it "being the Church."

"I wouldn't know what the rationale is for the church not being holistic—just having church and not being church," Caldwell said.[12]

Some laundromat customers in Arlington, Texas, are a bit wary when approached by a stranger who offers toys for children and free food. But they warm up quickly when they learn that Ron McLeroy is part of a street ministry that takes Bible lessons to unusual places.

"They pretty much open up to you quickly," says McLeroy, who drops in at coin laundries on their busiest days, Saturdays and Sundays. "It's good for the church to reach out past its doors into the community," he says. "Basically, it's taking Sunday school to the streets."

McLeroy is part of The United Methodist Church's Arlington Urban Ministries program. The laundromat ministry began in 1997. McLeroy took over the visits two years ago.

"Those are the ones that Christ talks about that the church is to reach, the poor and the needy," he says. "And I truly believe that we have to go outside the church to do that."

After he offers the food and toys, he gathers the children in the laundromat for a quick Sunday school lesson. He carries a felt board with figures to illustrate the story of Jonah and the whale. Using other teaching aids, he offers a sixty-second Bible lesson to adults.

Arlington Urban Ministries was started by First United Methodist Church and became an independent, nonprofit corporation three years ago. Besides the laundromat ministry, Arlington Urban Ministries offers financial help to families having trouble paying their rent and utility bills or buying groceries. It also offers pastoral counseling and crisis intervention for families.

Success can be seen on the smiling faces of children as they receive toys and treats from McLeroy, and as they take in a Sunday school lesson outside the doors of the nearest church.[15]

It was one of those "social action" churches.

There was a school for poor children, operated eleven hours daily. The church was the site of a "house of mercy" where room and board was given to destitute widows, unwanted orphans, and blind people.

A dispensary also operated out of the church, offering the free services of a pharmacist and surgeon to more than one hundred needy people every month.

Another phase of the church social program was a savings bank. Church members could deposit their money, knowing it would be used to help poverty-stricken families facing financial crisis. It was a kind of credit union.

In the church was a thriving bookstore.

This socially-conscious church was also a place of worship. Hundreds of people came on Sunday and during the week to hear the Gospel preached, sing God's praises, pray, study the Bible, and fellowship with other Christians.

Last but not least, the church provided living quarters for a traveling preacher named John Wesley. Between itinerant preaching missions, he lived in this church, as did his aging mother. It was the world's first Methodist church, established by John Wesley himself.

This church simply reflected the top-to-bottom social concern, which was woven into original Methodism's very soul and being.

This is why the influential *London Spectator* wrote: "The Roman church has been called the church of the poor; but that title of honor belongs quite as much, if not with a better right, to the Wesleyan body."[13]

Unwelcome is the prophet who thunders that God's justice will roll down like a mighty stream upon a church and a society characterized by violence and injustice. Unwelcome, too, is the other sort of prophet who declares the words of Jesus, "You must be born again" (John 3:7).

It seems a long, long way back to that compassionate first Methodist church that John Wesley established. But is it really "back"? Instead, is is not forward? Was not the original Methodist far ahead of us in comprehending the will of God and the nature of Christian faith as "close to the heart of mankind"?

To follow John Wesley would lead Methodism into new frontiers of perfect love. To follow him is to follow the one whom Wesley supremely loved and sought to obey, the Lord Jesus Christ. He was vitally concerned about the whole person's welfare in this world and in the next.[14]

Reaching Beyond Our Borders

The social witness of the Georges and of these churches is so like that of Wesley and the early Methodists. Every case represents a real witness for Christ that both reaches out to lost souls and addresses serious social challenges. Success is accomplished by giving that goes over and beyond apportionments and is independent of institutional concerns. This is "hands-on" ministry, engaging the realities of the world. While advocacy for political solutions may be important at times, the focus rests on real love manifested in a fallen world. These examples do not represent good works for the sake of good works, but rather good works for the sake of Christ and the making of disciples for Christ. Such ministry flows out of love for God, love for people, and out of apprentice-ship to Christ.

We hear Wesley's challenge to let our love for Christ and neighbor abound, extend, and overflow. We have witnessed how heartfelt, Spirit-driven ministry reaches beyond the borders of our personal lives and local church environment to the community and the world. We have glimpsed Wesley's concept of "the world is my parish."

Chapter Eight
All the World Is Our Parish

Pip: Methodists today are divided on what missions means. Some say it should be providing a variety of social services and engaging in political struggles; others, the preaching the Gospel of Christ. What do you think?

Wesley: God in Scripture commands me, according to my power, to instruct the ignorant, reform the wicked, confirm the virtuous. Man forbids me to do this in another's parish: that is, in effect, to do it at all; seeing I have now no parish of my own, nor probably ever shall. Whom, then, shall I hear, God or man?[1] I look upon all the world as my parish; thus far I mean, that in whatever part of it I am I judge it meet, right, and my bounden duty to declare, unto all that are willing to hear, the glad tidings of salvation. This is the work which I know God has called me to; and sure I am that His blessing attends it.[2] As the Methodist movement spread, it traveled far beyond my own small domain. At eighty-two I reflected on this truth. I was now considering how strangely the grain of mustard seed, planted about fifty years ago, has grown up. It has spread through all Great Britain and Ireland; the Isle of Wight, and the Isle of Man; then to America from the Leeward Islands, through the whole continent, into Canada and Newfoundland. And the Societies, in all these parts, walk by one rule, knowing religion is holy tempers; and striving to worship God, not in form only, but likewise in spirit and in truth![3]

THE MODERN MISSIONARY MOVEMENT

Early Predecessors

When the Wesleys journeyed to America in 1735, their desire was to convert the Indians and minister to the colonists. It was not a successful venture. John's despairing cry on his return was, "Who shall convert me? Who, what is he that will deliver me from this evil heart of unbelief?"[4]

Three years after his Aldersgate experience, John Wesley countered those who wanted to limit where he could preach by declaring that he saw all the world as his parish. This declaration began to be realized in Wesley's lifetime. Henry Carter recounts that as early as 1759, Methodism had won a footing in the British West Indies. Nathaniel Gilbert, a planter and politician from the island of Antigua, was converted after meeting John Wesley in London. He returned to Antigua and began working among the white settlers and the Negro slaves. After his death, John Baxter, a shipwright, continued the work. Again we mark the evangelical initiative of a layman.

In 1786, Dr. Thomas Coke sailed for Nova Scotia. The *Minutes* of 1791 include the appointment of preachers to seven islands under British sovereignty, and to Nova Scotia, New Brunswick, and Newfoundland.[5]

By the year of John Wesley's death in 1791, membership in the Society of the People called Methodists was: in Britain and Ireland, 72,476; in British Dominions in North America, 6,525; and in the United States, 57,621.[6]

By the late 1700s, the Church of England's older missions agencies, the Society for the Propagation of Christian Knowledge (SPCK) founded in 1698, and the Society for the Propagation of the Gospel (SPG), founded in 1701, had essentially abandoned evangelization.[7]

It was out of this barren mission field that God raised up two men—one an English Baptist, the other an American Methodist—who would receive a fresh vision from God regarding the Great Commission.

William Carey

Converted at the age of eighteen, William Carey made his living by teaching school during the week, mending shoes in the evening, and preaching in the Baptist church at Leicester, England, on Sunday. Early in his ministry, Carey became convinced that the Great Commission applied to the church of his day. He spoke out about this passion in his heart at every opportunity. On one occasion, he was shouted down by the chairman: "Young man, sit down! When God pleases to convert the heathen, he will do it without consulting you or me!"[8]

Though it imperiled his preaching career, Carey used every opportunity he had to teach and preach the implications of the Great Commission. In 1792, he wrote and published an eighty-seven-page booklet, *An Inquiry into the Obligations of Christians*, in which his thesis was "whether the commission given by our Lord to his disciples be not still binding on us."[9] As cited by H. T. Maclin, "This is believed today by many to be the greatest missionary treatise in the English language, a landmark in Christian history in its influence on subsequent church history."[10]

Carey's passion and persistence prevailed. At the 1792 Minister's Association, Carey again preached of his missionary vision, laying down two principles: expect great things from God, and attempt great things for God.[11] His sermon so moved the leader of the association that he put forward a resolution in the minutes that "a plan be prepared against the next ministers' meeting at Kettering for forming a Baptist Society for propagating the Gospel among the heathens."[12]

William Carey was the first to be asked to go—to India. His wife, Dorothy, refused at first to accompany him, but relented. Five months later Carey arrived in India with Dorothy, their four children, and two companions. He served for the next forty-five years, reaching the unreached with the healing Gospel of Christ. The modern Protestant missionary movement began.[13]

Six years after Carey sailed for India, the Church Missionary Society was founded by a few clergy and laypersons, notably John Venn, the rector at Clapham; and William Wilberforce, a member of Parliament and a close friend of Prime Minister William Pitt.[14]

Mission agencies today would likely thrive by applying the five basic principles of the Church Missionary Society:

1. Follow God's leading; nothing is more important.
2. Begin on a small scale.
3. Put money in the second place, not the first. Let prayer and study precede its collection.
4. Under God, all will depend on the type of men set forth. A missionary "should have heaven in his heart, and tread the world under his foot." Such persons only God can raise up.
5. Look for success only from the Spirit of God.[15]

Melville B. Cox

Melville B. Cox was born in 1799 and converted at the age of seventeen through the witness of a cousin. Two years later he felt God's call to preach and began his traveling ministry.

Cox wrote in his journal that he felt it was time to send missionaries to South America. Maclin wrote that the Council of Bishops also felt the need to send missionaries to the foreign field and was in the process of selecting the first mission area outside the United States. The Council eventually chose the newly formed nation of Liberia in West Africa. It had been founded in 1822 by the American Colonization Society as a place to send freed slaves from the United States who desired to return to their motherland. Some of these former slaves had become Christians; among them were those who had accepted Christ through the preaching of MEC circuit riders.[16]

At the 1832 General Conference held in Georgia, Bishop Elijah Hedding asked Melville Cox to consider going to Liberia as the church's first overseas missionary. Cox agreed, despite the fact that he had been ill with consumption for several years and had resigned from his last appointment for health reasons. Cox wrote in his journal that, "Liberia swallows up all my thoughts. I thirst for the commission to go. The path looks pleasant, though filled with dangers. Death may be there but I trust this would be well also."[17]

Cox left for Liberia, though his family and friends objected because of their concern for his health. The voyage took four months. He arrived in Liberia on March 9, 1833. Though Cox survived only four months in the harsh African climate, he neverthe-less established the first Methodist church on the African continent related to what is now The United Methodist Church. He began church school classes, founded schools, and an agricultural station. Prior to his departure, Cox said to a friend, "If I die in Africa, you must come and write my epitaph."

"I will," his friend replied, "but what shall I write?"

Cox replied, "Write, 'Let a thousand fall before Africa be given up!'"[18]

The passion for missionary outreach that burned within the hearts of Carey and Cox was ignited by the Holy Spirit in the hearts of others who were called to serve as part of the nineteenth- and twentieth-century missionary force. This was true for Methodists. By the early to mid-1920s, over 2,700 Methodists were serving Christ overseas—the largest number of missionaries from any denomination in North America.[19] The Great Depression and World War II curtailed the sending of missionaries abroad and many were recalled during this time.

MISSIONS TODAY

Our historical examination shows that when a passion for reaching a lost and hurting world for Christ is the foremost concern of the church, a vibrant social witness will surely follow. This was true for the early Christian church, the church of eighteenth-century England and nineteenth-century America, and holds true of the church today. Wesley and early Methodists reached out beyond the walls of the church to touch individual lives in prisons and coal fields—not only preaching the Gospel but relieving suffering and working for reform. The same can be said of Phoebe Palmer and countless revivalists of the holiness movement. Much suffering was relieved and injustice addressed. Most important, lives were touched by the transforming power of Jesus Christ.

A Recent Witness

Samuel Moffett is a renowned Presbyterian missiologist who spoke at the spring 2007 meeting of The General Board of Global

Ministries (GBGM). In remarks rarely heard at GBGM meetings, Moffett lamented: "The world is our parish, but we in America's mainline churches seem to be forgetting it. We are collapsing in on ourselves. We talk a global mission better than we do it."

Moffett noted that mainline Protestant missions agencies, of which GBGM is the largest, have had a numerically declining missionary force for forty years. He observed, "Fifty years ago mainline Protestant missionaries overseas outnumbered missionaries from evangelical churches by nine to four. Today, evangelicals outnumber mainliners by forty to three."

Without negating the importance of a strong social witness, Moffett challenged the board to a holistic understanding of mission that includes spiritual transformation.

A Faithful Witness

Dr. H. T. Maclin began missionary service with the Board of Mission of The Methodist Church in 1952. He accepted Jesus as Lord during his military service in World War II and felt strongly that the Lord had brought him through the war for a purpose. He and his wife, Alice, were challenged in a Sunday school class by an Australian missionary to take the Great Commission as Christ's word and be involved in His mission to the world. Maclin began his missionary service in the Central Congo Annual Conference and served in various capacities in Africa for twenty years. His work with the All Africa Conference of Churches not only took him all over the continent of Africa, but to the Middle East and Southern Asia as well. Shortly after Maclin returned from many years overseas, he became the field representative for Mission Development for the General Board of Global Ministries in the Southeastern Jurisdiction.

Maclin documented the change of mission focus he witnessed in the early 1960s while still serving under the General Board of Global Ministries. *In The Faith That Compels Us*, he wrote:

> Fewer missionaries were being sent out, and some who were retiring from their fields of service were not being replaced. The emphasis seemed to be slowly shifting from evangelism and evangelization to a variety of social services. To be sure, such services

were all necessary in any mission undertaking, especially in third-world settings. These were vital but auxiliary facets of Christian mission. Were they becoming substitutes for the primary task of Christian ministry and mission: that of calling people everywhere to personal trust and faith in our Lord Jesus Christ?[20]

As we go about the primary mission of the church to offer Christ as Lord and Savior we will naturally respond to obvious needs such as feeding the hungry, healing the sick and teaching the illiterate, Maclin asserts. But when the "old principle of the Gospel" is not observed, it is possible for the church to lose sight of its primary task. The promise that all things shall be added is not realized. When this happens, it is not only possible but likely the social witness of the church will lead to activism that opens itself to being partisan and political. The justice that is sought is elusive. In time, the pursuit simply becomes "another gospel."

Maclin is one of many United Methodist missionaries on the foreign field who have personally witnessed a shift in the church's emphasis on winning persons to Jesus Christ to an emphasis on social action. Others on various boards and agencies have documented the shift from a vibrant commitment to evangelism to a more activist political agenda. In fact, many who became active in the renewal movements within the denomination were once loyal missionaries and staff members of our boards and agencies.[21]

Strengthen the Missionary Force

Today, the Gospel continues to be taken to those who have not had the opportunity to hear and respond to Christ, but a shift has taken place. It is no longer the mainline denominations and United Methodists in particular who take the lead in offering Christ to the world. Just as church membership has dropped drastically in the mainline churches, so also the task of making disciples and reaching the lost for Christ has been taken up by others.

In the early 1990s, there were more Protestant missionaries from the United States serving overseas than ever before. But out of 40,000, only 9 percent came from churches that were members of the National Council of Churches (NCC). Of those, only 416 were from The United Methodist Church.[22] By 2007, the number had fallen to 403, including stateside missionaries.[23] The GBGM now has only 172 full-time United States missionaries in other countries.[24] This is in stark contrast to the missionary force in 1960, when the UMC was the largest Protestant mission agency in the United States with 1,580 missionaries.[25]

Much has been written regarding the decline of overseas missionaries, and many have attempted to provide reasons for this decline. Certainly we must acknowledge the growth of indigenous seminaries, churches, and other ministries that have taken the lead in many countries. Still, only one-third of the world's population professes to be Christian, and many have no clear knowledge of Christ and the way of life to which He calls those who accept Him as Lord and Savior.

EMERGENCE OF THE GLOBAL SOUTH

For some time, missiologists and Christian scholars have reported growth in real numbers of Christians in the world population. This growth has occurred primarily in the "Global South," which includes Africa, Latin America, and parts of Asia. In Africa alone, about 10 percent of the population was Christian in 1900, growing in 2000 to about 50 percent. In 2007, the figure rose to 477 million.[26] Missiologist Gerald H. Anderson described this growth in the Global South as the third great turning point in church history. The first turning point occurred when the first-century church, which started as an all-Jewish community, became overwhelmingly Gentile as the Gospel spread throughout the Mediterranean world. The second shift occurred when Christianity spread from the Mediterranean world to Europe.

No doubt the spread and growth of Christianity in the Global South can be attributed to missionaries who brought the Gospel and to faithful nationals who built and grew the churches. Since 1832, when Melville Cox was sent to Liberia in West Africa, Methodist churches have been established in more than sixty countries worldwide.[27]

Most of the people in the Global South are poor, and their countries are considered part of the undeveloped Third World. Professor and author Philip Jenkins says some western Christians have expected that the religion of their Third World brethren would be liberal, activist, and even revolutionary.[28] But these ideologies have not been widely embraced there; these ideas represent the perspectives of liberal, Western-educated clerics. Christians in the Global South are more likely to turn to a biblical understanding of spiritual warfare to address injustice. This is in stark contrast to the political solutions sought by many Christians in the West.

> Christians in the Global South are more likely to turn to a biblical understanding of spiritual warfare to address injustice.

The strength and exponential growth of these churches can be attributed to the fact that they are more generally conservative in beliefs and moral teaching than Christians in the mainstream churches of the Global North. These Christians take the truth claims of the Bible very seriously. Churches that have made the most progress in the Global South are traditional Catholics, evangelicals, and Pentecostal Protestants. The deep personal faith and communal orthodoxy these churches preach is founded on clear scriptural authority. They have experienced knowing God beyond intellect. They understand the reality of sin and take the moral teaching of the Bible at face value. These churches resemble the New Testament Church in many ways. They accept the supernatural acts of God as recorded in Scripture; rely on God to accomplish things that government often cannot; and adhere to the strong moral teachings of Scripture, as evidenced in their stance on homosexual practice. These churches identify with biblical stories, and the social realities of these stories are relevant to their lives. They have a deep understanding of atonement and worship in a revivalist and personal mode.

Jenkins says:

> If there is a single critical marker distinguishing the Christianity of the modern West from the New Testament world, it is the basic belief in the supernatural character of evil, which is manifested equally in sickness, repression, wickedness, and compulsiveness.[29]

Unlike many in post-Christian societies, Christians in Third World countries don't believe that evil can be dealt with by adopting a more tolerant view of our differences or making a deeper commitment to peace. They recognize that Jesus took evil very seriously. They do not see themselves as victims as such, but rely on faith and on the role of the individual, who is no longer a slave to destiny or fate. They rely on the power of Jesus.[30]

Persecution and martyrdom continue for many Christians in the Global South. Jesus' teaching that Christians can expect to be persecuted is a reality in the lives of many in Africa and Asia, including Sudan, Rwanda, China, and the Middle East. Suffering is experienced in ways that most of us in the West just cannot imagine. What is remarkable is that suffering does not lead individuals away from faith in God. Instead, it leads them to put little faith in government for their salvation. They can easily identify with the testimony of New Testament believers who lived within the Roman Empire.[31]

Because these Christians see the Bible as much more than a historical text, they passionately defend it. For them, the authority of Scripture is not something to be debated or passed off. They have not been silent when American and British clergy depart from biblical teaching, but rather, they take such clergy to task. Take, for instance, the clear statement made by an alliance of conservative Global South churches in response to the crisis in the Episcopal/Anglican Church:

> The unscriptural innovations of North American and some western provinces on issues of human sexuality undermine the basic message of redemption and the power of the Cross to transform lives. These departures are a symptom of a deeper problem, which is the diminution of the authority of Holy Scripture.[32]

Africa's Anglican archbishops vowed never to accept much-needed aid from western churches which support the ordination of gay priests. This was a courageous stand for these bishops who serve a church comprised of some of the world's poorest citizens. Yet, they remain faithful to the teachings of Scripture, refusing to compromise even when it entails sacrifice.[33] Their concern for the AIDS epidemic goes beyond rightly seeking medical care and options for those infected with the disease. They know ultimately God's Word holds the key to human sexuality and the problems that occur when commandments and prohibitions are ignored.

Archbishop Henry Luke Orombi of Uganda recounts his country's social realities before Christianity came. He says few of us can imagine a culture in which there was no written language and nothing to read. The Bible was the first book translated and read in that culture. The language of Uganda was recorded as a result, allowing an intellectual and spiritual development that was previously impossible.

Genuine personal and social liberation occurred as people embraced the Gospel and were freed from various superstitions. The Gospel was particularly freeing for women. But in Uganda, freedom for women did not come at the expense of marriage and children; instead liberation, flowing from the truth of Christ, strengthened this basic building block of society.

Perhaps the most profound societal change resulted from Christ's teaching on forgiveness. People moved beyond the idea of revenge based on blood ties, and embraced Jesus' admonition to love both neighbors and enemies. This was not a message based merely on newfound respect for all tribes and cultures, although that has occurred, but instead on Christ's teaching on forgiveness. The concept of forgiveness has been a powerful spiritual force in Uganda. Bishop Orombi shares:

The Gospel of Jesus Christ as revealed to us through the Word of God enables warring tribes to begin to coexist and to embrace neighborliness. Indeed the Word of God opened the way for the nation of Uganda to be forged. When evangelists from Buganda (in central Uganda) traveled to tribes in the east, west, and north, a new day dawned in our country. Instead of being armed with spears, they came armed only with the Word of God. Instead of a message of war and destruction, they delivered a message of Good News from the God and Father of our Lord Jesus Christ.[34]

Uganda is a modern-day example of the personal and social transformation that is possible when the Gospel is proclaimed. The message of Christ has brought the dawn of a new day in Africa.

Consider the Voices of African United Methodists

Nigeria is now one of the fastest-growing United Methodist conferences in the world. Overall, Africans now comprise about 25 percent of the membership of The United Methodist Church. The United Methodist Church in Nigeria has grown from ten thousand to more than four hundred thousand in just fifteen years![35]

A strong emphasis on biblical teaching and evangelism has fueled rapid church growth in many parts of Africa. Many within United Methodism believe that God could use the faithful, biblical witness of the African churches to renew American United Methodists' commitment to doctrinal faithfulness and evangelism.[36] At no other time were the voices of our African brothers and sisters heard more clearly than at General Conference 2004, when they boldly asked The United Methodist Church to stand firmly on its position regarding homosexual practice, which they perceived to be directly related to the teaching of Scripture. Listen to these voices:

Tshibang Kasap 'Owan (North-West Katanga):

We have received teaching from our missionaries on marriage. Before Christianity arrived in Africa we practiced polygamy. And the Christian teaching that we received taught that there should be marriage between one man and one woman. And this was Christian marriage. We Africans, we accepted this teaching, and we became Christians. Now we are hearing another message in this General Conference, speaking of homosexuality. . . . We respect our culture and the good things in our culture and we do not want to become drawn into this problem of homosexuality. . . .

Many within United Methodism believe
that God could use the faithful, biblical
witness of the African churches to renew
American United Methodists' commitment
to doctrinal faithfulness and evangelism.

Muland Aying Kambol (South Congo):

My name is Aying. I am a pastor in southern Congo. If The United
Methodist Church today is passing through a time of confusion, our
children will live through a time of destruction in the church. . . . I
am discouraged when I see so much time being spent to talk about
this sin, when to me, it is very clear that this is sin.

Yemba Kassongo (Central Congo):

The church needs to speak with a clear voice. . . . That is why I
challenge and urge all the conferences of Africa and here in
America to move for concurrence on this Minority Report because
the church has a mission that God gave it. If America will not do
it, God will raise the bones to do it.

The United Methodist Church in America is blessed to have
this missionary witness from our African brothers and sisters. Their
commitment to remain faithful to scriptural teaching and evangelism is a great source of encouragement for the church. For this
reason, and more, any discussion of making the United States a
separate Central Conference, removed from the other Central
Conferences, is anathema in the hearts of many United Methodists.

The African Church and Poverty

While faithfulness to Gospel proclamation and biblical authority is not a cure for all of the social and political problems in Africa and elsewhere in the Global South, it produces transformed lives through which God can work in behalf of spiritual and physical needs by the power of the Holy Spirit.

At the spring 2007 meeting of the Council of Bishops, the first ever held outside of the United States, African bishops reported both good news and challenging news. The good news pertained to the explosive growth in conversions which equals membership. The challenging news pertained to the fact that The United Methodist Church in Africa faces poverty of economics, education, and health. African Methodists "recognize they have spiritual problems as well as worldly problems . . . the African people are a religious people so they search . . . they have a sense of hope," said West Angolan Bishop Gaspar Joao Domingos.

Presenters at the bishop's meeting explored root causes for the problems of African poverty and offered varying solutions. Some called for outside help, and others felt African Methodists should be a part of the solution. Bishop Joao Machado said that Africans must find their own means to solve their own problems. In actuality, it takes both outside help and African effort to resolve serious poverty issues. Professor Rukudzo Marupa warned that there is no instant answer to poverty in Africa, and that the church alone cannot solve poverty.

Here, the Spirit of God is moving, the Gospel is being preached, and lives are being transformed. It is the ideal climate for a Wesleyan social witness to emerge.

Learning Our Lesson

What lessons should we learn from Christian brothers and sisters living in the Global South? We can rediscover an uncompromised adherence to the authority of Scripture and realize that this leads to positive results for individuals and cultures. Also, we can take seriously the Bible's teaching on evil and on the sinfulness of human nature. Embracing a biblical worldview will provide a clear understanding of the real sources of evil, the importance of spiritual resources, and understanding that secular and political options alone cannot address the root causes of evil.

We cannot deny that for our brothers and sisters in the Global South, a faithful, biblical witness may bring persecution. We should expect our church leaders to speak up boldly when our Christian brothers and sisters are persecuted. But often it appears that our boards and agencies have more to say in defense of the rights of people groups who have rejected the Gospel than they do for our fellow believers who suffer persecution. We should remember Paul's admonition to the Galatians: "Therefore, as we have opportunity, let us do good to all, especially to those who are of the household of faith"(6:10).

The faithfulness of the churches in the Global South is exemplary. Their testimony stands in contrast to those who would use the church for theological malpractice and for their political agenda. We are reminded by Christians in the Global South that a true prophetic witness is based upon clear scriptural, moral, and ethical truth.

HOLD FAST TO THE ETERNAL

Justice will always be a concern of the church. Yet, today, there are those who hold an agenda for peace and justice as the primary mission of the church. Their concerns, however genuine, are defined by a political view that the West has become overtly dominant, lusting for power out of arrogance and callousness to the needs of the rest of the world. Many believe that the Gospel of Christ has little or no significance in today's culture. To them, Christianity is accepted as one religious option among many—one they perceive as dangerous if adhered to in exclusive or fundamental ways.

Believers who live in the Global South would beg to differ. They have learned it is not political posturing in the name of the Gospel, but the Gospel itself that holds the keys for all humanity to achieve victory over sin and death. They understand that it is only through Jesus Christ that we have real hope for achieving justice in this world. Indeed, we see in the southern-hemisphere

Church a high view of the Bible that protects them from the secular and moral compromises within the North American church. Many of the struggles within United Methodism would disappear if scriptural authority were taken as seriously as it is in the Global South.

Chapter Nine
Reclaiming the Wesleyan Social Witness: Offering Christ

Pip: If United Methodists want to reclaim the heart and soul of your message, what would that be?

Wesley: Salvation by faith! Everyone who believes in Him may not perish but may have eternal life . . . This truth is the foundation of all our preaching, and it must be preached first and foremost.[1]

Pip: Then our Christian experience is primarily personal?

Wesley: It is that . . . but, let no one be self-deceived. It is crucial to keep in mind that the kind of faith which fails to produce repentance, love, and good works is not genuine living faith. Instead, it is dead and entirely deficient.[2]

REVISIT THE FAITH OF THE SAINTS
Re-establish a Christian Worldview

From its inception, Christianity has been the most powerful, life-changing religion ever known. Beginning with the announcement of His birth by angels, and through His life of complete obedience to the

Father, manifestation of divine power, unbridled love for humanity, unjust but necessary death on a rugged cross, and resurrection from the dead and ascension into heaven, Jesus Christ offered salvation to the whole world. Christians have been given the opportunity to share this good news, bringing millions to personal faith in Jesus Christ as Savior. Yet, we are also commissioned to proclaim Him as Lord of all. Our *Book of Discipline* states, under The Mission and Ministry of the Church, "The United Methodist Church affirms that Jesus Christ is the Son of God, the Savior of the world, and the Lord of all."[3]

What does this truly mean? *In How Now Shall We Live?*, Charles Colson writes:

> Genuine Christianity is more than a relationship with Jesus, as expressed in personal piety, church attendance, Bible study, and works of charity. It is more than discipleship, more than believing a system of doctrines about God. Genuine Christianity is a way of seeing and comprehending all reality. It is a worldview.[4]

Colson did not discount any of the components of Christian faith, he simply wants us to understand that it must affect every aspect of our existence.

Colson speaks of Jesus' astonishing and absolutely true claim, "I am the way and the truth and the life" (John 14:6). Christ is indeed the beginning and end of all things. Nothing exists or has meaning apart from him. Accepting Jesus' claim brings us again to the reality that "Christianity cannot be limited to only one component of our lives, a mere religious practice or observance, or even a salvation experience. We are compelled to see Christianity as the all-encompassing truth, the root of everything else. It is ultimate reality."[5]

Of course, this thinking lines up well with that of John Wesley, whose Christian ethics were based on a distinctly biblical worldview. He taught that we could not know truth apart from God's revelation of it through Scripture and through the person of Jesus Christ. He wrote: ". . . we are to look for no new improvements; but to stand in the good old paths; to content ourselves with what God has been pleased to reveal; with 'the faith once delivered to the saints.'"[6] Wesley knew that this worldview would affect our personal and social lives. He said, "Instead of teaching men that they may be saved by a faith which is without good works, without 'gospel-obedience and holiness of life,' we teach exactly the reverse, continually insisting on all outward as well as all inward holiness."[7]

Therefore, as we revisit the faith once delivered to the saints, we find that it is well-balanced and far more encompassing than many may have realized. Colson says:

> Our calling is not only to order our own lives by divine principles but also to engage the world. . . . We are to fulfill both the great commission and the cultural commission. We are commanded both to preach the Good News and to bring all things into submission to God's order, by defending and living out God's truth in the unique historical conditions of our age.[8]

Recall the Faith of Methodism

Since its inception, Methodism has modeled the kind of Christian worldview Colson speaks of. Even before their conversion, John and Charles Wesley performed many works of charity and justice as participants in the Holy Club, which they initiated at Oxford. It was only after their personal conversions, however, that their lives and their ministries had the spiritual vitality to affect the religious and social structure of England, and eventually America and beyond. Historians speak of the far-reaching effects of the spiritual awakening under John Wesley.

In his thirteenth discourse on the Sermon on the Mount, Wesley anticipated the process by which Methodists would bear witness to the world. Wesley encourages us to answer the question, "What is the foundation of my hope?" Is it orthodoxy, church membership, the principle of "doing no harm," a good conscience, participation in the ordinances of God, or good deeds? He implores us, "Renounce all hope of ever being able to save yourself. Place all your hope on being washed in Christ's blood and cleansed by his Spirit."

Today, The United Methodist Church is divided over the proclamation of the Gospel and social justice ministry. Dr. Steve Harper calls us back to our Wesleyan roots when he writes:

In our own time the cause of social concerns goes under many names and grows out of differing philosophies. It is important to understand Wesley's social contribution in light of the ideologies that promote social reform today. The key for doing so is the remembrance that Wesley's social concern was inextricably rooted in the Christian faith. He was fundamentally an earnest Christian, who sought through a variety of means to effect the redemption of fallen humanity.[9]

If The United Methodist Church is to move into the twenty-first century with power and relevance, we need to discard the cultural and intellectual influences that failed in the past centuries, yet still linger. Most important, we who have professed Christ have to take seriously the totality of His teachings. Both salvation and social justice must be rooted in the truth claims of Christ.

It is true that real oppression needs to be addressed by the church. But if examples from the previous century have taught us anything, it is that mere campaigns for justice do not bring about true transformation. For example, throwing money at a problem such as the World Bank has tried to do in Africa, where the money has often ended up in the hands of despotic rulers, showcases the result of "justice" gone sour. But on the other hand, we have documented that when the Gospel has been preached in Africa and elsewhere, lives are transformed and social justice also advances.

What we do want to consider is what faith in Christ says about who He is and who we are in Him. For herein lies the answer to society's problems. If the church does not faithfully proclaim the greatest story ever told, who will?

Both salvation and social justice must be rooted in the truth claims of Christ.

TRUST GOD FOR NEW BEGINNINGS

A New Beginning Through Repentance

Yet, before we can be faithful to our mission of proclaiming the Gospel, becoming disciples, and engaging in social witness, the church must understand its need for God's grace and mercy. We need to acknowledge where we have lost our way and seek to follow after Christ anew. Christ made it clear that to follow Him requires repentance (Luke 13:1–9). The apostle Paul was one of the most successful individuals of his day in proclaiming the Gospel and making disciples for Christ. Yet, before his ministry for Christ began, believing himself devout and acting for God, he persecuted the early believers. This is a powerful example for the church today.

Dr. James Heidinger articulated The United Methodist Church's need for repentance in his book *United Methodist Renewal: What Will It Take?* He wrote:

> Though we talk about reversing our membership decline, we seem to be more embarrassed than repentant about our losses. The truth is we are not yet repentant about our spiritual and theological condition. . . . where is the anguish over the loss of two million members and over the decimation of our church schools which saw attendance drop from 4.2 million to 2.1 million in the last two decades? Where is the broken heart over the loss of an entire generation of young people—that next generation of United Methodists we've failed to reach because of insipid youth ministries and preoccupation with theological fad?[10]

Membership loss was at 2 million in 1988 when the book was written. It now stands at 3 million plus.

No doubt, there is so much more to repent of on the part of church members of all theological, political, and social persuasions. Who of us can claim that we have been totally faithful to Christ in our personal devotional life; in our lifestyle before the world; and in our loving compassion for the bodies, souls, and spirits of the lost? Wesley spoke of those who understand the deeper grief that leads to repentance:

Of course, God enables repentance, which is nothing other than a deep sense of the absence of good and the presence of evil. . . . Whatever so-called "virtues and good works" one may have, they are of no advantage as means of salvation. Until we trust in Jesus, we are still children of wrath and under the curse.[11]

It is this awareness of lostness and powerlessness, both for ourselves and for others, that moves us to repentance and intercessory prayer.

If we are to remain faithful to our mission to make disciples of Jesus Christ and reclaim our social witness for Christ, the church will have to come to terms with the influence of secular ideologies, political agendas, or elitist pietism. We must not only acknowledge our failures, but also repent of our mistakes. This was powerfully stated by Leicester Longden in the 2007 Consultation on Judicial Council Decision 1032:

We have lost our way as a church. The astonishing gift of our tradition . . . has been laid aside because we have been dazzled by other things. The spell must be broken. We must "come to ourselves" and repent. We must learn again how to "watch over each other in love." To recover the gifts of our heritage as a people with high expectations for disciples, we must do more than merely agree to develop common practices of accountability. We must recover a passionate seeking after holiness, "seeking the power of godliness" as stated in our historic General Rules. This kind of recovery is not something we can engineer as a quadrennial emphasis. It will require repentance. We must begin to think of recovery as a return to health, as the opening of our eyes, as the healing of a sickness, and most importantly, as a divine gift. This gift will be the fruit of repentance.[12]

If the church is to accept this divine gift, it will require repentance. We must humbly acknowledge that "all have sinned and fall short of the glory of God" (Rom. 3:23).

A New Beginning Through Proclamation

Prior to Jesus' public ministry, John the Baptist preached a message of repentance. When Jesus began His earthly ministry, He did so in His home synagogue in Nazareth, claiming for Himself the words of Isaiah that He was the one sent to "proclaim good news to the poor . . . freedom for the prisoners . . . and the year of the Lord's favor." Matthew tells us that Jesus began to preach "repent, for the Kingdom of heaven is near" (3:2 NIV).

Jesus preached a new relationship with God that would be brought about through His own life, death, and resurrection. It was the gift of Jesus' life that set aside the penalty of the law and made it possible for the finger of God to write that law on our hearts. So it is through the life, death, and resurrection of Jesus that the reign of God broke into human existence and people experienced signs of the kingdom. Jesus was the key. The change in heart and transformation of the soul and the subsequent transformation of culture and society made possible through Jesus' life and death cannot be overemphasized.

In the same way, the disciples proclaimed the Kingdom of God, and hearts and lives were changed as people received a message of God's grace and repented. Proclaiming the Gospel not only gave birth to the church, but spoke justice into the world in a way a political program could not have accomplished. In time, the unjust political reality of the early church did change. The Church's faithful witness to Christ brought about the abandonment of pagan religions and Christianity became the official religion of the Roman Empire. When we proclaim the Gospel, our message must center on Christ; He is the Word of God proclaimed. This is where the pursuit of justice begins. True liberation begins in the heart of every individual.

A New Beginning for Our Social Witness

In his book *Good News About Injustice,* Gary Haugen gives us insight into how God sees injustice and oppression, while also emphasizing the necessity of retaining Bible teaching as we respond to human need:

> True liberation begins in the heart of every individual.

Biblical Christians understand that Christ has called us to be his witnesses to the uttermost part of a very dark world—a dark world of injustice. Preparing our minds for action in the world means coming to grips with the notion that the world into which we are sent as salt and light is a world that needs salt and light precisely because, among other things, it is full of the corruption and darkness of injustice . . . .

And while the kingdom of God will be complete only in the coming of Christ, today our great joy and privilege is to work as co-laborers with the Creator in extending his kingdom over one more life, one more family, one more neighborhood, one more community. The people of God will find in Christ the compassion and courage to engage the call to justice, for we know God promises that [those] who do not "become weary in doing good . . . will reap a harvest if we do not give up" (Gal. 6:9).[13]

Haugen refers back to the great achievements in humanitarian reform and social justice in the West during the nineteenth century, noting that the abolition of slavery, prison reform, the establishment of hospitals and schools for the poor, women's rights, opposition to prostitution, and the fight against child labor were causes led by evangelical Christians. Many evangelical Christians in the twentieth century neglected social witness. Yet Haugen says there is hope: ". . . Christ has not neglected us, and now he calls us to recover the ministry of justice that once was ours."[14]

Carl F. Henry described the balance we should all long to reclaim:

If the church preaches only divine forgiveness and does not affirm justice, she implies that God treats immorality and sin lightly. If the church proclaims only justice, we shall all die in unforgiven sin and without the Spirit's empowerment for righteousness.[15]

We must seek both. Our Wesleyan forebears modeled it so well. John Wesley's greatest desire was the saving of souls, but he understood that this entailed loving people enough to minister to their needs and liberate their bodies even as God liberated their souls.

Our confusion has often come as the church embraced political, social, or secular answers to human need and failed to be the church with its own God-given answers. This has been evident as many church leaders, members, boards, and agencies have embraced the equivalency of all world religions that inhibits the proclamation of Jesus as the one and only Savior of the world; advocated for social justice programs that make victims of the poor; aligned the church with agencies that are pro-abortion and that affirm homosexual practice; and advocated for a narrow, biased political agenda on complex social issues.

The '60s approach of focusing on the "sinful structures" of society has been devastating to the witness of the church, for it moves individuals from a place of personal responsibility to victimization and from need to entitlement. It is difficult to proclaim the Gospel of hope and transformation to those who are confirmed and convinced of their hopelessness, passivity, and resentment. A church that follows this course finds itself offering only social services—or justice—paid for by the state. The price of sin, paid for by the blood of Jesus Christ, goes unheralded. This approach also seriously neglects the Bible's teaching on the power of forgiveness. Christ offers forgiveness to all who repent and teaches us, in turn, to go and forgive others. This spiritual principle is a powerful healing reality in the lives of individuals and cultures. But the power of forgiveness has too often been exchanged for ill-conceived social prescriptions.

In some of our General Conference resolutions, the mission of the church has been tied to the goals of secular institutions. In others, we have advocated programs that have little or no relevance to our mission. Indeed, some resolutions have gutted or ignored altogether the truth of the Gospel. At future General Conferences, will we pass more such ill-conceived legislation? Or will we take an honest soul-searching look at how we have perceived social justice, rejecting that which has failed and returning to policies and legislation built on a biblical worldview? It is important for the church to remember that at the heart of every need is the need for a Savior. As we sort out issues of justice, we will have to come to terms with what has promoted real justice and social progress as well as what has done more harm than good.

A New Beginning

The issues that divide the church today, whether it be homosexuality, how we address the poor in our midst, or the acceptance of truth claims of other religions, primarily find expression and implementation through the social witness of the church. Many have brought to our attention the serious theological issues at stake. But although these divisions are rooted in deep theological concerns, these issues find their way into the life of the church through our social witness.

In today's highly polarized political environment, those who see the church advocating their personal political commitments and resulting theological stands will raise no objections. Others, who believe the very witness of the Gospel is betrayed, will continue to hold the church accountable. Or, like so many before them, they will simply leave our ranks—as individuals or as entire church bodies. This has been the reality for the mainlines for decades now. Activist causes, particularly when they appear to sideline or work against the very foundations of the Gospel, will not serve the church or humanity.

During His earthly ministry, Jesus proclaimed that the kingdom was at hand, yet not of this world. Did He care about the suffering and injustice into which He was born? There is no doubt. But, when offered the kingdoms of this world with all of their political power and resources, Jesus rejected the offer (Matt. 4:1–11). His kingdom was not of this world.

Jesus passed His message on to His disciples and gave them authority to preach the Gospel, accompanied by the power of the Holy Spirit. The Church was born and its mission became that of proclaiming what Christ Himself had taught and preached. The church's mission is to proclaim and not to govern. In Dietrich

Bonhoeffer's words, "The peculiar character of the Church . . . lies in the fact that in the very limitation of her spiritual and material domain she gives expression to the unlimited scope of the message of Christ . . . The Word of God, proclaimed by virtue of a divine mandate, dominates and rules the entire world. . . ."[16]

What about this message, and what about justice? How did Jesus address injustice? He went to the cross.

The justice Jesus proclaims and the justice that prevails when His life, death, and resurrection are accepted as truth is available today. In the early church, during Wesley's time, at the settling of our own country and the frontier, presently in the Global South, and in times and places that go unmentioned, the Gospel message proclaimed has within it the power to transform evil at every dimension of our personal and social lives. What could be more unjust than the failure of the church to offer the world the trans-forming power of the Gospel?

Justice begins in our dealing with one another. In that sense, it flows from the bottom up, not the top down. Justice proceeds from the heart of each and every individual, and from there it flows to all of life. Efforts to impose or coerce justice have no power to stem the root cause of injustice. Only the totality of the Gospel can effect such change.

Jesus tells us that in this world we will have tribulation. There is no utopia apart from the coming kingdom. But He also tells us to "be of good cheer, I have overcome the world"(John 16:33 KJV). The United Methodist Church has a rich heritage of proclamation and social witness that has gone far in the healing of individuals and the healing of the nations. As we seek to reclaim and

What could be more unjust than the failure of the church to offer the world the transforming power of the Gospel?

recommit to the proclamation of Christ and the incumbent mission and social witness, we join our Lord to "proclaim good news to the poor . . . freedom for the prisoners . . . and the year of the Lord's favor" (Luke 4:18–19 NIV).

Chapter Ten
Responding to God

Pip: We've shared a lot about the history of Methodism and the problems we're facing, but what advice would you give us as we move forward?

Wesley: I would say, respond to God. The most important thing is to know the way to the Kingdom. That should be the supreme desire of every person. When you consider how to have an effective social witness, you must realize that society can be changed only when individuals have been transformed through the Holy Spirit.[1] Remember the words of our Lord describing the two grand branches of righteousness. "You shall love the Lord your God with all your heart, and with all your soul, and with all your mind. This is the first and greatest commandment," the first and great branch of Christian righteousness. The second branch of Christian righteousness is closely and inseparably connected with the first branch: "You shall love your neighbor as yourself."[2]

RENEWAL THE WESLEY WAY

Wesley scholar Dr. Steve Harper wrote *John Wesley's Message for Today*, in which he examines how Wesley's teaching continues to be a source of inspiration and guidance for Christians today. Harper answers the question, "How would John Wesley seek to renew the church if he were alive today?" He says Wesley would:

- Urge all people to personally experience Christ [Justification by faith became the touchstone of the Methodist revival.];
- Urge Christians to greater degrees of discipline ["The soul and the body make a man; and the spirit and discipline make a Christian."—Wesley];
- Encourage believers to gather in groups [The lack of relational ministries in the church has contributed significantly to a loss of spiritual vitality.];
- Call us to a renewed appreciation for the sacraments [It is of grace, not of ourselves that we are what we are . . . the sacraments are constant reminders of this truth.];
- Emphasize that Christ be offered to everyone [Wesley would call us to a ministry to the total person in the total society, all over the world . . . stressing the need for such a ministry to be distinctively related to the name and spirit of Christ.].[3]

RECLAIM THE MEANS OF GRACE

John Wesley was a strong proponent of God's grace. He believed that grace goes before our conversion (prevenient grace), is active at the time of our conversion (converting or saving grace), and continues at work throughout our Christian lives (sanctifying grace). Wesley taught that practical Christian growth comes through the means of grace. Harper writes:

The "means of grace" was a particular term in Protestant and Roman Catholic circles to describe the specific channels through which God conveys grace to his people. Wesley never limited

God's grace to these "means," he only believed that the means of grace were the normal (ordinary) ways that God enabled the believer to grow in grace.[4]

Wesley divided the means of grace into two categories: the "instituted" and the "prudential." The instituted means of grace are those practices that Christ specifically commanded. They include the Christian sacraments, prayer, searching the Scriptures, fasting, and Christian conversation [holy conferencing]. The prudential means of grace are those practices that Scripture and experience show to be wise and prudent for Christian disciples. There are three headings for these practices—doing no harm, doing good, and using all the ordinances of God [attending private and public worship].[5] Wesley did not believe the means of grace had power within themselves, but were merely things that God uses to accomplish His work in our lives.[6]

Let's look more closely at the five instituted means of grace.

Prayer

Wesley listed prayer as the first means of grace. He called prayer "the grand means of drawing near to God" and felt that all the other means should be mixed with prayer.[7]

Harper shares Wesley's serious view of the importance of prayer, saying that Wesley called the lack of prayer the common cause of "the wilderness state" (a sense of spiritual dryness and purposelessness). Wesley also said that the lack of prayer in one's life cannot be made up for by any other means.[8] Harper writes that Wesley urged people to follow his example of disciplined, regular prayer.[9]

Prayer is the very powerful means of grace that the church has neglected to its peril. When the founder of Gospel for Asia, K. P. Yohannan, first visited churches in America, he was astonished to find how few people came to the prayer services. In India, the spiritual darkness and pressing need drove people to pray. We too are in spiritual darkness and have great need, but have not yet realized our serious need to pray.

Prayer strengthens our personal relationship with God—but it is more. It is the means through which God's Holy Spirit can speak to us, sharing God's heart for us and for the world. In the place of

> Prayer is the very powerful means of grace that the church has neglected to its peril.

prayer, God, through the Holy Spirit, speaks to us of "sin and righteousness and judgment" (John 16:8). Churches that are growing, sharing the Gospel, and doing works of mercy and justice are, almost without exception, praying churches.

Wesley encouraged both personal and corporate prayer, and so must we. If we are sincere about reclaiming our Wesleyan heritage and about witnessing the kind of change this must bring to our congregations, we will pray. In the words of Matthew Henry, "When God intends great mercy for His people, the first thing He does is to set them to praying."

Searching the Scriptures

The second instituted means of grace is what Wesley called searching the Scriptures. Wesley declared that he was a man of one book, knowing that it provided all he needed to "land on that happy shore." Wesley aided followers by compiling notes for both the Old and New Testaments and making them available at reasonable prices.[10] He also advocated regular and thorough Bible study times, and wanted believers to understand and apply God's Word to their lives. He wanted readers to ask, "What does this mean for me?" and "How can I put the truth of Scripture to work for the good of others?" In this way, the Bible served as an important means of grace.[11]

While most Christians readily accept the importance of Scripture's role in personal Christian growth, not all readily understand how the Bible is to inform our worldview as it relates to justice. Gary Haugen, in *Good News About Injustice*, powerfully makes this point:

Jesus calls us to be witnesses of his love, truth, salvation, compassion and justice . . . "to the ends of the earth" (Acts 1:8). Again this is the unique biblical hope that Christians can offer a world groaning under the heartache of injustice and oppression: God has compassion on the victims of injustice all over the world, among all people, without favor or distinction. We will, through our act of compassion, give witness to our belief that what the Bible says is true, or not.[12]

Under the section on Scripture, *The Book of Discipline* states:

Our standards affirm the Bible as the source of all that is "necessary" and "sufficient" unto salvation (Articles of Religion) and "is to be received through the Holy Spirit as the true rule and guide for faith and practice." (Confession of Faith).

Scripture is a means of grace. We need to ask, "How well do we avail ourselves of it?"

Widespread Biblical Illiteracy

In a time when the majority of Americans (some estimate up to 85 percent) consider themselves to be religious and aligned to organized faith, only a small percentage of these individuals are biblically literate. What does this say about the church? Are we educating our members in basic biblical theology? Are we giving our members a deep understanding of our basic Christian beliefs? Are we teaching the Bible and our own religious tradition as precious truth, or just an option among many other religious truth claims?

A recent Barna Research Group study answered these questions. The report indicates that a large share of people who attend Protestant and Catholic churches have adopted beliefs that conflict with the teachings of both the Bible and their church. The study revealed that while a high percentage of respondents still believe in the Trinity, that humans have an eternal soul, and that the Bible can be understood by the average person, other areas did not rate as well.

- Six out of ten Americans reject the existence of Satan;
- A large majority of Americans believe that Jesus committed sin when on earth;
- Half of all adults surveyed believe that being or doing good will merit a place in heaven;
- A whopping 74 percent believe people are born neither good nor bad, rejecting the Christian doctrine of original sin; and a shocking 44 percent contend that the Bible, the Koran, and the Book of Mormon are all different expressions of the same spiritual truths.[13]

George Barna concluded:

Over the past twenty years we have seen the nation's theological views slowly become less aligned with the Bible. Americans still revere the Bible and like to think of themselves as Bible-believing people, but the evidence suggests otherwise. Christians have increasingly been adopting spiritual views that come from Islam, Wicca, secular humanism, the Eastern religions, and other sources. Because we remain a largely Bible-illiterate society few are alarmed or even aware of the slide toward syncretism—a belief system that blindly combines beliefs from many different faith perspectives.[14]

Biblical Illiteracy Prevalent Among Youth

In 2005, the Bible Literacy Project published a two-part study which found that both high school and university English teachers believed that Bible knowledge gave students an ability to understand classic and contemporary works. The teachers also reported that fewer than one-fourth of their students were biblically literate.[15] Part two of the study was conducted by The Gallup Organization, who surveyed teens between the ages of thirteen and eighteen, and confirmed only a minority of American teens were Bible literate.[16]

If a survey were taken of United Methodist teens, would their basic Bible literacy be higher than the study's findings? The study found that even teens who identified themselves as born-again and evangelical lacked in-depth Bible knowledge.[17]

David Gelernter, senior fellow in Jewish Thought at the Shalem Center, believes, "Our churches, our synagogues, and all other institutions that revere the Bible must do better." He says that the young adults, especially college students, are ripe for a religious revival along the lines of another Great Awakening. "They are empty, spiritually bone dry, because no one has ever bothered to give them anything spiritual that is worth having. Platitudes about diversity and tolerance and multiculturalism are thin gruel for intellectually growing young people."[18]

Are we in The United Methodist Church guilty of giving our young members "thin gruel"? Mission studies that teach our young people about environmental and geopolitical issues are hardly giving them knowledge of Scripture, much less the theological and spiritual formation they need. It is in the church where people learn to please God first and foremost. This, in turn, means they will live a life in the wider society that promotes righteousness and justice. Are we training the emerging generations scripturally, theologically, and morally? Or are we merely attempting to mold their political sensibilities?

Young people today are bombarded with messages of sin, death, and despair that come through any number of avenues. Young people and adults alike are still looking for the way to live their lives; they want to know the truth, not explain it away; they want to live in the light. Perhaps they, like Wesley, want to know what it really takes to land on that happy shore. The church has the privilege and responsibility to teach them the way, the truth, and the life, from God's Holy Word.

The Lord's Supper

John Wesley received communion about once every four or five days. He exhorted early Methodists to practice constant communion, which meant being present for Holy Communion at every opportunity. On occasion, Wesley led Methodists from their preaching houses to local Church of England parishes so that they might receive the sacraments. When Methodists were no longer welcome at these altars, Wesley found other legitimate ways to provide the Lord's Supper for them.[19]

Why did Wesley put so much emphasis upon the sacrament of the Lord's Supper? He believed the experience was not just a symbol, but a chance to receive the grace of God. He didn't believe in transubstantiation, but he did believe that Christ was present in the service.[20]

To Wesley, the Lord's Supper was not only a means of strengthening the lives of believers, but also a sacrament that had a converting potential. The invitation to the Lord's Table was an open one, yet had specific expectations of those who came. The Service of Word and Table IV in *The United Methodist Hymnal*, page 26, provides the traditional text from the rituals of the former Methodist and former Evangelical United Brethren churches:

Ye that do truly and earnestly repent of your sins,
and are in love and charity with your neighbors,
and intend to lead a new life, following the commandments of God,
and walking from henceforth in his holy ways:
Draw near with faith, and take this Holy Sacrament to your comfort,
and make your humble confession to almighty God.

This opened the way to salvation to any who came and made this vow with genuine commitment. Many within the church today advocate a different kind of open table, one that says anyone may come, whether they earnestly repent and intend to live a new life and follow God's commandments or not. Those who are in willful violation of the teaching of Scripture and the doctrinal standards of the church should refrain from coming to the table until they are ready to make "a humble confession to almighty God," and accept repentance and newness of life.

Fasting

Wesley believed that fasting mediated grace to enrich the Christian life. Early in his ministry, he observed Wednesday and Friday as fast days, following the practice of early Christians. Later he fasted only on Friday and encouraged his followers to do likewise. For Wesley, fasting began after the evening meal on Thursday and continued until tea on Friday afternoon. This time was given to prayer, devotion, and spiritual matters.

While Wesley sometimes engaged in longer periods of fasting, he deemed this shorter time sufficient as an ongoing means of grace. He did not view fasting as mortification of the flesh, but rather as a time set apart to and for God.

Fasting is a biblical principle. It has in all ages and among all nations been much used in times of danger, mourning, sorrow, and afflictions. From the time of Moses, fasting was a recognized Jewish practice. Individual and corporate fasts were observed, such as the fast called by Queen Esther as she prepared to go before the king (Esth. 4:15–17); or the fast King Jehoshaphat called all of Judah to when they faced a formidable enemy (2 Chron. 20:1–13).

While Jesus did not institute a particular fast, He assumed that His followers would fast when He was no longer with them (Luke 5:33–35). The condition He made was that any fasting be sincere and discreet (Matt. 6:16–18).

In this day, when our church faces formidable challenges within and without; when we continue to lose members and experience internal division and compromise; in this day when we do not always "do justice, love mercy, and walk humbly with our God"; do we need to consider fasting as a much-needed means of grace? As our personal lives grow cold and we "lose our first love," would a personal, regular time of fasting help us find grace to help us in our time of need? As foreign as fasting may seem to our modern-day thinking, it is a discipline we should rediscover.

As foreign as fasting may seem to our modern-day thinking, it is a discipline we should rediscover.

Christian Conference

United Methodists occasionally hear the term "Christian Conferencing" used in relation to Annual or General Conference or other church-related events. It is not a twenty-first century term, and we probably are a bit confused by it. The practice it represents has experienced a resurgence of interest in our day.

"Christian conference," as Wesley called it, referred to group fellowship in the Christian context. He considered it an important means of grace for believers. Harper says this means became the primary instrument of early Methodist renewal. Wesley organized believers into bands, classes, and societies for their continuing nurture. In 1743, he organized these groups into the United Societies, a movement within the Church of England. Methodism remained as a "little church" within the larger body until shortly after Wesley's death.[21]

Wesley put much store in these groups as a means of grace. On one occasion, he remarked, ". . . preaching like an apostle without joining together those that are awakened and training them up in the ways of God, is only begetting children for the murderer."[22]

Wesley was also convinced that wherever this dimension of discipleship was lost, Methodism would cease to be a vital movement. As Wesley saw deterioration within the group structure as the years passed, he warned against it:

> Never omit meeting your Class or Band; never absent yourself from any public meeting. . . . The private weekly meetings for prayer, examination and particular exhortation has been the greatest means of keeping and confirming every blessing that was received by the word preached and diffusing it to others. . . . Without this religious connection and intercourse the most ardent attempts, by mere preaching, have proved no lasting use.[23]

Harper believes Wesley's concern has proven true in today's UMC, as "the lack of relational ministries in the church has contributed significantly to a loss of spiritual vitality." This should give us pause.

The small group, or cell church, model has gained in popularity in the United States since the 1970s. For large churches this model brings people together in fellowship, prayer, and support in ways the larger body cannot replicate. In the current cell-church movement, there are healthy and unhealthy elements. It would seem wise for leaders and churches within The United Methodist Church to revisit its own Wesleyan roots in the area of Christian conference, study present-day options, and find biblical models that can help revitalize the spiritual lives of individuals and renew the spiritual vitality of our churches.

RESPOND TO GOD

There is truth and power in the voices of those who have contributed to this effort to call United Methodists to the reclaiming of their Wesleyan social witness by offering Christ:

Dr. James V. Heidinger II:

Yes, we need a new atmosphere within United Methodism. And our bishops must help here. They must call for and exhibit themselves a new high standard of theological integrity for our church as well as for our seminaries. . . . If The United Methodist Church is to recover its Wesleyan doctrinal heritage, pastors must challenge the church's institutional patterns and priorities. And laity will need to join them in doing so. These patterns and priorities will not be easily changed, for they are firmly established in our church structures.[24]

Dr. H. T. Maclin:

While the primary task of missionaries is to offer Christ as Lord and Savior, virtually all who are personally involved eventually come to realize that other forms of services are badly needed, indeed required, as an ancillary part of what missions is all about—reaching out to people wherever they are and touching their lives by responding to obvious needs such as feeding the hungry, healing the sick, and teaching the illiterate. To close one's eyes to such conspicuous human need is simply not possible. The soul must be saved; the mind must be renewed; and even the body is to be redeemed. The Gospel of Jesus Christ is designed to meet the needs of the whole person.[25]

Dr. Christopher T. Bounds:

The United Methodist Church in her mission and ministry, in the recovery of her social witness must once again commit herself to the task of preaching the "Word of God," of proclaiming the Gospel. While proclamation is not the only means by which God's redeeming and transforming grace is made available in the world, it is central. True social change, true inculcation of the Kingdom of God cannot happen apart from sharing the Gospel. In this regard the church must recover what is clearly stated and indicated in her doctrine of the Church, summarized in her doctrinal standards.[26]

Dr. H. O. "Tom" Thomas:

In conclusion, John Wesley and the Methodists are exemplary in Christian history as authentic proponents of both evangelical faith and social love, justification by faith and good works, inward and outward religion, the "personal" and the "social." Through their own personal experience of the love of God and the love of humankind in justification and sanctification, they offered to any who would receive the possibility of full redemption from ills of soul and body. Holding together both personal pardon and social love, the higher goal of the salvation of souls was the deepest motivation for social mercies of bodies.[27]

Across the years, God has raised up many within Methodism to call this denomination to renewal, accountability, and faithfulness to our Articles of Religion, Doctrinal Standards and to scriptural Christianity. Books could be written about these faithful United Methodists, both well known and hardly known, who loved this church and gave much to secure its heritage for the next generation. We honor the ministries of these who have gone before us, and respond to God's call through them.

Bishop William R. Cannon, a beloved bishop of The United Methodist Church, addressed a conference in 1990 from the perspective of an imaginary conversation with Wesley. A noted Wesley scholar, Bishop Cannon often asked himself what Wesley would do or say under similar circumstances. He felt Wesley would have this to say:

> The radical difference between you United Methodists and me is that you make social concerns the primary objective of your ministry, which I never did. Social and political matters were only incidental to me. I did not even realize I was a social reformer at all. I looked on myself as an evangelist, trying to win souls to Christ and to prepare people for heaven. . . .[28]

What of us as United Methodists? What is our chief goal?

Perhaps some, like Wesley, are seeking the same assurance of salvation that drove him to "win souls and prepare them for heaven." The assurance of our salvation through faith in the atoning death of Jesus Christ for our sin is a mark of Methodism.

For others, there may be the desire to repent and align one's life with Scripture in order to realize the holiness of heart and life our heritage advocates.

The goal of some may be to apply with fresh vigor the means of grace Wesley identified: prayer, Bible study, the Lord's Supper, fasting, and Christian conferencing, finding in these the deeper life to which we are called as faithful United Methodists.

Pastors and church leaders may determine the need to provide studies on United Methodism's Wesleyan heritage, focusing on Wesley's sermons, the Articles of Religion, and the Doctrinal Standards of the church.

For all, there is the need to awaken from our lethargy—and from our spiritual and social neglect—to reclaim our heritage as those who, like Wesley, are evangelists of the finest order—evangelists who do not neglect the total needs of spirit, soul, and body. We need to do no harm, do good, and use all the ordinances of God at our disposal.

It is time for those who are alive in Christ to reclaim the level of commitment that was instrumental in spreading scriptural holiness across the land. Methodism was the early bearer of this message of salvation and sanctification of heart and life. If our witness in this area is to be effective, it must go beyond a local church jurisdiction, or conference, to encompass the whole denomination, calling it to reclaim the Wesleyan social witness—by first and foremost offering Christ. Using this book, along with the study questions for each chapter in the appendices, provides a beginning point, offering a catalyst for further study and action.

Oh, the potential for United Methodism to recover its heritage and to bring spiritual awakening and a powerful social witness to the nation and the world.

Lord, make it so!

Appendices

Appendix A
Study Questions

These questions can be used for group or individual study.

CHAPTER ONE

1. The beginning of this chapter focused on the Methodist legacy through John and Charles Wesley. What theological discoveries did these two young men make in their early years, then later as they encountered the Moravians and engaged the teachings of Martin Luther? How did this impact the message they shared and the lives they touched?

2. Some have discarded a Gospel of personal transformation for a social gospel intent on the transformation of society. How did the Wesleys view these two facets of Christian faith? Did one take precedence over the other?

3. Some of the ways the social gospel is misunderstood and misapplied have been identified. What elements of a Wesleyan-style personal and social gospel can we apply to assist us in making wise legislative and ministry choices?

4. Give your personal response to the following statement: If our social witness is to be more than just "the religion of the world," then we must have a clear conception of "true religion." If we

have not experienced the love of God through Jesus Christ, and are unwilling to share the transforming Gospel with those we serve, how can our acts of love deliver God's highest promise to humankind?

5. Respond to the only quote from Wesley regarding social holiness: "The Gospel of Christ knows of no religion, but social; no holiness but social holiness." According to the context in which this statement was made, how do you interpret it? How does it apply to social witness?

CHAPTER TWO

1. Read the following statement from *The United Methodist Book of Discipline*. What relevance does it have regarding the Gospel witness and social witness of the church?

   Our struggles for human dignity and social reform have been a response to God's demand for love, mercy, and justice in the light of the Kingdom. We proclaim no *personal gospel* that fails to express itself in relevant social concerns; we proclaim no *social gospel* that does not include the personal transformation of sinners (par. 49).

2. Read the following mission statement of The United Methodist Church. How should this relate our Gospel witness and social witness? What does it mean "to make disciples of Jesus Christ"?

   The mission of the Church is to make disciples of Jesus Christ.
   —Par. 120, *The Book of Discipline*

3. Does the contemporary church view social witness as a means to present Christ to the world, or as an end in itself?

4. Reflect on the principles identified in this chapter. How can they inform the legislative process of The United Methodist Church and help shape its future?

CHAPTER THREE

1. How does the social gospel movement of the late nineteenth and early twentieth centuries compare with the Wesleyan social witness which was an integral part of the initial Methodist movement?

2. The theological identity of the Methodist Church was greatly affected by social gospel theology. What were some of the theological components of the social gospel? How was sin viewed under this ideology? How was the concept of salvation affected?

3. What were some of the concerns that liberal-to-moderate voices expressed about the social gospel's influence upon the Church?

4. Give your description of "fundamentalism." Is this a negative or positive term to you? Why?

5. What were the fundamentals of the faith that John Wesley adhered to and called Methodists to embrace? Do you find that these fundamentals provide specific doctrinal standards United Methodists can embrace today with confidence?

CHAPTER FOUR

1. Discuss the theological differences between liberals, moderates, and conservatives as identified in this chapter. Where do you place yourself?

2. If the social gospel has failed, why is this so?

3. What is your personal assessment of the feminist movement? Are all forms of feminism bad? What barriers, if any, do you perceive as preventing the full inclusion of women in mission and ministry?

4. According to your understanding, has the involvement of the National Council of Churches (NCC) and the World Council of Churches (WCC) in social justice issues helped or hindered the various causes they have championed?

5. Dr. Chris Bounds reflects hope for the Church if it will return to its primary mandate: to proclaim the Gospel of Jesus Christ. Do you agree or disagree with Dr. Bounds's assessment? Discuss why or why not.

CHAPTER FIVE

1. What were the key defining factors that caused Methodism to grow and produce fruit as it was transplanted to America?

2. Membership decline began as early as 1850 in Methodism. What factors caused this membership loss? What are the factors that contribute to membership loss today?

3. What is the primary mission of the Church? Is our denomination effectively fulfilling this mission?

4. Some United Methodists say it does not matter when the bishops or boards and agencies of the church make radical or partisan political pronouncements. Do you agree? Why or why not?

5. What guiding principles should help shape the Church's political/social witness?

CHAPTER SIX

1. Have you, as a United Methodist, found the ten concerns in Dr. William Abraham's list on pages 71 and 72 relevant to your own thinking about United Methodism?

2. Do the facts about women under the section "The Reality for Women" come as a surprise to you? Are their gains yet to be made in behalf of women? Identify them.

3. Do the facts about men under the section "The Reality for Men" resonate with your awareness of the needs of men and boys? What gains need to be made for men and boys? How can the church help?

4. How do you answer the question, "Has the church neglected the care and nurture of this basic institution (the family)?" How do current statistics about the family confirm and/or deny your assumptions?

5. Do you agree with the statement, "One aspect of the social witness of the church that should be rethought is the tendency to advocate serous social issues exclusively in terms of 'rights.'" Why or why not? How does the Bible address "rights" and "responsibilities"?

6. Did Wesley "go easy" on the poor? How about the rich?

7. Talk about the eternal loss that is realized when the Church fails to proclaim the Gospel of Christ and to model a faithful social witness.

CHAPTER SEVEN

1. What did Wesley mean by his concern that the Methodist movement could become "a dead sect, having a form of religion without the power"? Do you think this has happened to Methodism? Why or why not?

2. Rank the following three items based upon your personal understanding: personal holiness, social holiness, personal salvation. Would that order change based upon the premise of this chapter?

3. What has been your experience, or your impression, of the balance between Gospel proclamation (i.e., evangelism and missions) and a viable social witness in the churches in which you have had membership or leadership?

4. Share the most meaningful Gospel transformation you have ever witnessed for yourself or another individual. Share the most meaningful social witness ministry you have engaged in or heard about.

5. Is it possible to separate Gospel proclamation from social witness and still be the church described in Scripture or represented in early Methodism?

CHAPTER EIGHT

1. Do you view the decline of United Methodist mission personnel overseas as a cause for concern? What do you see as the root cause for this decline?

2. What do you consider the primary objective of mission activity? How important is evangelism? How important is social witness?

3. When you hear the term "peace and justice," what comes to your mind? How do you think the boards and agencies of The United Methodist Church interpret these terms?

4. How does it strike you that United Methodists from the Central Conferences provide a strong faithful witness to the standards of biblical Christianity and to the current doctrinal standards of our church at General Conference and beyond?

5. What are some ways the North American church can better embrace the witness of the Global South church, and also minister justly to that region of the world?

CHAPTER NINE

1. How would you define "the faith once delivered to the saints"? (Jude v. 3)

2. What is a "Christian worldview" and how does one acquire it?

3. Do you concur with the premise that repentance is essential for a new beginning for us as individuals and for our church? Discuss.

4. How can we assure that our social justice witness is shaped by a biblical worldview? Where does Scripture, tradition, reason, and experience come into play in determining an orthodox, Christian worldview?

5. How do you respond to the evangelistic nature of John Wesley portrayed throughout this book? Does it cause you to want to share your faith with others?

CHAPTER TEN

1. Which of the means of grace appeals the most to you? Why?

2. How has this study aided you in understanding the Wesleyan social witness and its relationship with offering Christ?

3. Has this study helped identify areas where corrective measures are needed for our denomination? What are those areas and what consequences do you see if we do not make changes?

4. What is your next step in responding to God? How would you like to see your local church respond? How would you like to see the denomination respond?

The Historical Wesleyan Witness
H.O. "Tom" Thomas Jr.

Sarah Peters was titled by John Wesley "lover of souls." By self-confession, Sarah said she could "not rest day or night, any longer than I am gathering in souls to God." Gifted to seek and save the lost, she was also a constant visitor to London's Newgate prison. She tirelessly cared for and ministered to prisoners. Skimping on her meals and petitioning government officials for pardon on prisoners' behalf, she fell victim to a jailhouse fever and died.

Sarah Peters exemplifies the Gospel the Methodists proclaimed. It was a Gospel synchronizing the profoundly personal and the ardently social. This paper sets forth the nature of John Wesley's theological balance in which the two grand Scriptural doctrines of evangelical, personal faith and zealous social love, cooperated in tandem to offer a counteractive to human sin and misery. We will consider how justification by faith and sanctification and their meaning and relationship necessitate a Gospel comprehending faith and good works, both personal and social. The paper will then illustrate how John Wesley and early English and American Methodists' faith expressed concretely in four ways love for neighbor.

GRAND SCRIPTURAL DOCTRINES

Definitions

John Wesley compressed into a thimble the very essence of true religion. Put variously, he summed it up generally as "the love of God and of all mankind; the loving God with all our heart and soul and strength, as having first loved us," or "our fellowship with the Father and with the Son." He said he longed to see established in the world "a religion of love and joy and peace, having its seat in the heart, in the inmost soul, but ever showing itself by its fruits."[1] This true religion was "the experimental knowledge and love of God, of inward and outward holiness."[2]

Perhaps his favorite Scriptural distillation, "faith thus working by love," encompassed all he envisioned in the general summaries above.[3] Further, it incorporated into one phrase the two, overarching grand scriptural doctrines implicit in these summaries that make explicit the gospel he preached: justification by faith and holiness.[4] Indeed, justification and sanctification constituted the full salvation John Wesley consistently preached for some fifty years. Holding these together as two convenient handles is key to the Wesleyan witness. If one goes wrong here, the Wesleyan witness will go awry.[5]

For example, critics then and now have argued variously that Wesley retracted his teaching on sanctification when he began preaching justification, and, contrarily, that he reneged on justification later in the revival when he emphasized sanctification.[6] Moreover, contemporary scholars are wont to submerge justification into sanctification, so that it is swallowed up into what seems to result as an overriding message of sanctification. None of these were Wesley's nor his peers' understanding of the message he preached. The best view of Methodist theology is the one Wesley vigorously insisted on a year before he died. He said he still witnessed the same confession he had had for fifty years, holding consistently together both justification by faith and holiness.[7] One's view in this regard affects not only one's understanding of the nature of Wesley's message but also whether or not and in what regards his message was personal and/or social.

So, the grand Scriptural doctrines of justification and sanctification testify to the dual nature of his theology and provide the basis for a proper understanding of its personal and social elements. A brief definition of what John Wesley meant by the terms "justification" and "sanctification" illuminates what he meant by "true religion." Wesley defined justification by faith as "a deliverance from guilt and punishment" of sin "by the atonement of Christ actually applied to the soul of the sinner now believing on Him."[8] It is "present pardon and acceptance with God." God's acceptance comes through faith. This faith of acceptance is a sure confidence in the meritorious cause of one's acceptance, Jesus Christ's atoning death on the cross.[9] Faith is the divine, inner conviction that "Christ loved me and gave Himself for me."[10] In the instant one has faith, one is justified. The "faith" part of the summary expression, "faith working by love," is short for justification by faith.

The second grand Scriptural doctrine, sanctification, commences once a sinner is justified by faith and accepted of God. The "working by love" part of the expression "faith working by love" is short for sanctification. Once the justified experiences the pardoning God's love and knows He who "was offended is now reconciled," love for God is poured into one's heart.[11] A new birth ensues that entails a radical transformation of the heart from love of the world to love of God and others. This is the beginning of sanctification, or holiness.[12] From this beginning, holiness generally gradually develops such that the saved sinner grows in grace, more and more dies to sin, and is "zealous of good works, both works of piety and mercy." Development continues until with a single, pure intention one loves God "with all our heart and soul, and our neighbour as ourselves."[13]

Relationship

Now, turn for a moment to consider with John Wesley the place, value, and relationship of justification and sanctification. Keeping these in their proper places ensures a proper perspective of the Wesleyan concern for personal salvation and social concern. Justification and sanctification can each, separately or together, be called salvation.[14] Both are equal constituent parts that must be held together in tension and equilibrium. Neither is to be belittled or to gain ascendancy over the other. Both complement salvation. Wesley said, "They [Methodists] take care to keep each in its own place, laying equal stress on one and the other."[15] They maintained them with equal zeal and diligence. Wesley consciously desired to avoid the extreme of those who, on the one hand, spoke well of justification but were ignorant or confused about sanctification; or of those, on the other hand, who were unacquainted with justification and confounded it with sanctification. Indeed, some in the Protestant Reformation tradition in Wesley's own day as well as in modern times (often evangelicals, but not exclusively, e.g., towering twentieth-century theologian Rudolf Bultmann), view justification as the summit of religion. There are others who, taking a more Catholic perspective, mix justification and sanctification.[16] In our own day, various liberation theologies and the social gospel very popular with clergy and church leaders give short shrift to justification by faith and personal aspects of sanctification.

Rounding out his views on the value of justification and sanctification as the inextricable co-essentials of the Gospel, Wesley drew on the apostle Paul's statement in 1 Corinthians 13:13. He noted that as glorious and honorable as faith is, love (sanctification) is more excellent. Justification by faith is the door of religion, but sanctification is the room, religion itself. Justification is the means, sanctification the end. Logically prior, justification by faith is the handmaid of love and the grand means of restoring humankind to the love from which he was fallen. Justification encompasses the relative change of what God does for us; sanctification, the real change of what God does in us. That is, justification brings about the reversal of relations between God and humankind, enabling sanctification to transform both the believer's heart and human nature.[17]

When considering John Wesley's social witness, keep in mind his assumption that true religion includes justification and sanctification as the one, grand possibility for fully redeeming humankind from all evils, both of soul and body. Not just justification or sanctification alone, but both working together in their proper relation, sequence, and place. The social witness of love through outward, good works and acts of mercy subordinates itself to the larger end of true religion. Unequivocally, the higher end to be kept in view in doing works of mercy is the saving of souls from death.[18] The ultimate aim of Wesley's social ethic is individual renewal. This is the precondition for social renewal.19 Among church leadership and our clergy, this principle needs urgent recovery.

Be that as it may, the true religion of love of God and of humankind is twinned companions and coadjutants working in tandem to achieve virtue and happiness across the land. Only the love that flows from and is experienced in justification by faith shows fruits, which work no ill to neighbor and issue in every kind of beneficence. As Wesley said, there is no other "strait way to the religion of love" but through justification by faith.20 Justification is God's transcendent dimension touching the inner person that results in the love that has a social concern. Likewise, justification by faith must express itself in love, when given opportunity, to prove itself authentic reconciliation with God.

True religion, both the love of God and of all humankind, none other, is "the medicine of life, the never-failing remedy, for all the evils of a disordered world, for all the miseries and vices of men."21 This love of God and the love of all humankind is what Wesley described as "the religion we long to see established in the world."

Personal and Social

Building upon this foundation, let us address a relevant issue and the subject of ongoing debate into the twenty-first century. In what way is the Gospel John Wesley preached both personal and social? Our *Book of Discipline* says United Methodists "proclaim no personal gospel that fails to express itself in relevant social concerns; we proclaim no social gospel that does not include the personal transformation of sinners."22 Are the two in harmony? Let me immediately alleviate any anxiety by saying John Wesley's theology is both personal and social.

Consider the meaning of the word "personal." One dictionary defines "personal" as what pertains to, concerns, or affects the individual person as opposed to others or the general community.23 If John Wesley's theology is anything, it is personal through and through. The power of his preaching was his offer to persons in his generation genuine religion, available to each person. Not until the Gospel became personal to him did he understand this.

Experiencing the very personal nature of the Gospel was integral to his own transformation. The Moravian leader August Spangenberg asked him soon after he landed in Georgia, "Do you know Jesus Christ?" Wesley could only respond for the generality of humankind, "I know He is the Saviour of the world." Spangenberg pressed him, "Do you know He has saved you?" Not until two years later, in the spring of 1738, could he answer a personal yes. Then the Gospel became real within his own heart. He testified famously, "I felt I did trust in Christ, Christ alone for salvation; and an assurance was given me that He had taken away my sins, even mine, and saved me from the law of sin and death."[24] To ignore or attempt to rationalize away the personal elements in his theology is to eviscerate it and miss it entirely.

There are several particular ways the Gospel he preached is personal. First, though the universal reality of all humankind is in some ways affected by the Gospel, the grand Scriptural doctrines, by nature, are distinctly directed to and meant to address the individual person. Each and every person is accountable before God. Each person stands utterly guilty before God. Sin is one's own and no one else's. Likewise, each and every person—even me, even you—is particularly loved, chosen, and marked out to be the especial recipient of God's gracious beneficence. Of course, each person must choose to receive the grace by faith. Just as Jesus singled out the hemorrhaging woman in a crowd, each person is treated as though he or she alone and no one else is the focus of Jesus Christ's atoning work.[25]

Second, the Gospel is personal in another way. In fact, the Gospel is doubly personal in that it is revealed to the individual person by a Person. The transcendent, personal God who was "in Christ, reconciling the world unto himself" is personally present to the individual person. John Wesley said, "The knowledge of the Three-One God is interwoven with all true Christian faith; with all vital religion." That is, one cannot be justified or sanctified without knowledge of the Three-One God.[26] God in Jesus Christ confronts the sinner regarding his or her sin. God in Jesus Christ reveals Himself individually to the penitent sinner and speaks personally to him or her—and us—words of pardon. Each person who will believe may hear his Voice say specifically to him or her, "Thou, even thou, art reconciled to God." God "hath sent forth the Spirit of his Son into my heart, crying 'Abba, Father.'" John Wesley envisaged this intimate, antiphonic conversation between God and child, "Thou art the man! I want thee for my Lord."[27]

Third, the Gospel is personal in that the faith of justification and sanctification is by its very nature an inner, super-sensual personal awareness. John Wesley declared, "The root of religion lies in the heart, in the inmost soul. . . ."[28] For him, personal religion has its seat, its epicenter in the inner being of a person—the heart and soul. True, Christian religion is the apprehension of the objective reality of God in one's inner experience.[29] Pure and undefiled religion arises when God touches the interior faculties of heart and soul.[30] The great work God does, He does in the soul.[31] Saving faith is an event that happens to the person in such a way that the person knows the Transcendent God is engaging him or her. It is an inner, suprasensuous apprehension that Christ loved and gave himself for them. The person becomes conscious that he or she is the focal point and object of God's redeeming activity in the here and now.[32] So, the Gospel is personal in at least two ways: it is directed to the person by the transcendent Person and experienced within a person.

Having said this, the Gospel is also social. The term "social" has a number of important shades of meaning that may lead conversing persons into misunderstanding when using the same term in different ways. A clue to two important ways John Wesley used it is gleaned from the only place in his many volumes of works where he used the term, "social holiness." This term is often quoted and equally misapplied today; Wesley used in the preface to his list of poetical works. He wrote: "The gospel of Christ knows of no religion, but social; no holiness but social holiness."[33] In the preface, he was countering the Christian mystics' notion of holiness that withdraws itself from society into entire seclusion from others. This monastic view tried to build on the foundation of justification by retreating in order to purify the soul. This Wesley roundly denounced.[34]

To the contrary, believers are nourished when they abide in Jesus Christ and are knit together in assembly with one another.[35] When he speaks of holiness as "social," he is arguing that persons grow in holiness and into the measure of the stature of the fullness of Christ when in mutually edifying social company and fellowship. Wesley's passionate commitment to Methodist society and class meetings is renowned. As other Wesley scholars observe, his point in speaking of social holiness was not to draw a distinction between the personal and social gospel as is done in contemporary American theology. Rather, he was saying that Christianity cannot subsist at all without society, without living and conversing with other men.[36] Therefore, "social" means that which is capable of being associated with others and marked by mutual relations enjoyed in the company of those with kindred interests.[37]

The second important sense in which he uses the term "social" is again in debate with the mystics. He reacts to the mystics' idea of solitary religion as the way to achieve sanctification. The mystics' way did not trouble itself with outward works. Wesley said, "If thou wilt be perfect, say they, trouble not thyself about outward works. It is better to work virtues in the will." Moreover, the one who attains true resignation separates him or herself from outward things.[38] Wesley repudiated this view that distanced itself from outward, good works. "Solitary religion is not to be found there in the gospel of Christ," he declared. The one who loves God loves others. The one who loves his or her brethren as Christ loved them, cannot but be "zealous of good works."[39]

Outward, Good Works Necessary

Upon God's pardon through faith in the merits of Jesus' atoning death, the love of God is immediately poured into the believer's heart. The "working by faith" piece of John Wesley's favorite expression "faith working by love" is actualized. Sanctification commences. Inner renewal occurs and genuine love for neighbor is given so the believer loves his or her neighbor as his or her very own soul. Methodists receive a love in which they love, as Wesley said, "every soul which God hath made," and every person "on earth, as our own soul." When this "love is shed abroad in his heart . . . the love of neighbor sweetly constrains him to love every child of man with . . . a love of benevolence, of tender goodwill to all the souls that God has made."[40] Believers are zealous to relieve "the distress of our neighbour, whether in body or soul."[41] The incomparable motivational force of God's love was personally revealed to Wesley. He confessed he sought this love of true religion for many years— to no avail. But when coming under its full conviction, he declared it to all.[42]

The outworking of justified faith in love is such that it cannot but put forth branches of outward obedience.[43] True, living faith was necessarily productive of all good works and all holiness (sanctifica- tion).[44] The child of God is like an apple tree. If the tree has life, it will produce apples. Good works are joined to faith as an effect is joined to its cause. The relationship is so direct, if one willingly neglects good works, he or she cannot reasonably expect that he shall ever be sanctified. Moreover, one cannot grow in grace, retain the grace received, or continue in the favor of God without faith working itself by love.[45] John Wesley proclaimed, "It is incumbent on all that are justified to be zealous of good works."[46] He declared, "None are finally saved but those whose faith 'worketh by love.'"[47]

Furthermore, since every one when he or she believes is sancti- fied, this sanctification must be both of heart and life. Sanctification of heart and life must express itself in inward and outward good works. Namely, love produced by faith has both an inward and an outward aspect. The inward aspect of sanctification comprehends a personal, inherent change in the inward tempers, qualities, virtues, and dispositions, and in the outward aspect a change of personal behavior that keeps the commandments and does good works. These outward good works include both works of piety and works of mercy. Works of piety take in such things as public, family, and private prayer; studying Scripture; fasting; and receiving the Lord's Supper. Works of mercy flow from a love of neighbor and relate to both bodies and souls of persons, including feeding the hungry; clothing the naked; entertaining the stranger; visiting those who are in prison, sick, or afflicted; instructing the ignorant; and comforting the feebleminded, among other things.[48]

Wesley is truly a model theologian in Christian history who dili- gently tried to keep together and in proper relation both evangelical faith and love, justification by faith and good works, inward and outward religion and, what one could say today, the personal and social gospel. He lamented it was Satan's work to separate inward from outward religion and set them at variance with one another.[49]

Two Misunderstandings

Two comments follow from John Wesley's view of social holiness. They may help clear up contemporary misunderstandings. First, there is a common misapprehension that justification pertains to the personal, and sanctification pertains to the social in the Wesleyan witness. This is only partly correct. For Wesley, justification is personal. Sanctification is both personal and social. Indeed, he stated uncompromisingly that social sanctification that consists only of outward ceremonies and forms and the doing of much good is a counterfeit outward religion. He said, "Holiness can have no existence till we are renewed in the image of our mind. It cannot commence in the soul till that change be wrought . . . till we are born again."[50] This inner work is the heart part of his phrase "holiness of heart and life."

He deemed sanctification a "poor farce and a mere mockery of God," "bare external religion," and a "round of outward duties" without the inner personal experience of divine reality within.[51] Whether one attends regularly public and private worship, prays, partakes of communion, studies the Bible, visits the sick and imprisoned, feeds the hungry, engages practically in the struggle against poverty, works to transcend racial and color boundaries, commits to overcoming violence and the nonproliferation of arms, takes steps to affect the environment positively, or whatever else it may be, if the personal dimension of sanctification has not begun, holiness is an empty charade and worthless. One may do good, and have no religion at all.[52]

Instead, Wesleyan holiness has every bit as much to do with the inward person as with outward, social actions. Outward good works are the outworking of an inner, personal work of God in the soul. Moreover, the personal and social aspects of sanctification are in a synergistic, cooperative relationship. They act together to increase the effect of one another. Personal growth in holiness coacts with outward good works increasing love and good works. Increased zeal for outward, good works coacts with personal holiness further deepening personal, holy virtue.

Second, when Wesley wrote about social holiness, he meant something different from what church leaders often today mean by the social gospel. Social gospel advocates erroneously equate true religion with social redemption from the collective sin of institutions and social structures.[53] Neither is social holiness a liberation theology, in which biblical texts are interpreted and given the meaning of some sociopolitical ideology like Marxism, socialism, feminism, etc.[54] Neither is salvation to be viewed as liberating society from the political-economic structure of the capitalist system or collective oppressed groups from racism, chauvinism or homophobia.

Contemporary clergy have assumed it is the bounden duty of social holiness to concentrate Sunday morning sermons on such themes. Doing so is not in accord with John Wesley's theology or admonition to the clergy. He did allow that now and then, when appropriate, a preacher might defend a political figure. Nevertheless, he was clear: "It is our main and constant business to preach Jesus Christ, and him crucified."[55]

Practicing Love for Neighbor

Now, having laid down this theological backdrop to the social witness, we shift gears to highlight prominent, concrete ways that John Wesley and the early English and American Methodists' faith expressed love for their neighbor. Are these the only ways Methodists demonstrated love and concern? By no means. Wesley addressed tracts, wrote letters, and instituted rules in the societies that expressed love and concern toward ills that straddle the line between the personal and social, such as the use and abuse of spirituous liquor, the avoidance of paying tax on goods, luxurious dressing, the use of money, prostitution, visiting the sick, medical illnesses, and the revolutionary war. Nonetheless, the following are prominent illustrations of how Wesley was constrained by the love of God to lead the Methodists in outward, good works.

Wesley's love for the poor was a common denominator by which many of his concerns are divisible. There was definite reason to love the poor. In his day, English society was structured like a socioeconomic pyramid. With vast distinctions between rich and poor, there were a few at the top and many at the bottom. Poor laborers received ten pounds a year in wages. The prime minister spent fifteen pounds a night just for candles to light his home.[56] Laboring people's strength was sapped for little reward and little thanks. Everyone below the income of a skilled craftsman was undernourished. Women and children were particularly vulnerable. To the bulk of the population, toil, deprivation, uncertainty, and suffering were constant daily facts.[57] When John Wesley visited on his preaching rounds, he found people he described as "half starved with cold and hunger, added to weakness and pain. But not one of them unemployed."[58]

Adding to the fact of his personal experience with his family's chronic indebtedness, Wesley's sensitivity to the plight of the poor was stimulated as an Oxford student. He realized he was not able to help a thinly clad woman in winter because he had spent money decorating his rooms.[59] Later, he regulated Methodist Society life with the poor in mind. In 1741, one of the Society rules was that the class leader take an offering each week toward the relief of the poor.[60] Society members were urged to bring clothes and a weekly penny for needy Methodists. A bronze slot was put into Bristol's New Room chapel door with these words, "Give to ye poor. Happy is he that hath mercy on the poor."

Wesley also directed society lifestyle in accordance with the deprivation of the poor. He said society members should avoid pearls, gold, and costly apparel because the "more you lay out on your own apparel, the less you have left to clothe the naked, to feed the hungry, to lodge the strangers, to relieve those that are sick and in prison. . . ."[61] Though they did not endure, he built poorhouses for destitute widows and children.

While he went begging for the poor more than once, his begging at age eighty-two in ankle-deep snow in London for five consecutive days at Christmastime is striking.[62] Wesley's counsel to Methodists is to be remembered: "Put yourself in the place of any poor man, and deal with him as you would God should deal with you."[63] The symbiotic relationship between the personal concern for soul and social mercy for the body was evident in his ministry to the poor. With penetrating insight, he noted the hope of saving the souls of the poor from death was one of the strongest incentives to all acts of bodily mercy.[64]

Loving one's neighbor and outward holiness also entailed doing what Jesus said to do, to visit those in prison. In the eighteenth century, prison was an extremely harsh reality. Laws were not very discriminating. One could be executed for murder as well as for pinching (stealing) handkerchiefs. Nineteen-year-old Elizabeth Hardy was sentenced to hang for stealing goods worth fifty dollars! At the last moment, she got a reprieve. Aiming simply to confine people, many prisons were small and overcrowded. They could be damp and cold. Half of the prison population was debtors—like John Wesley's father. When William Smith observed occupants in 1776, he saw them scantily clad in a "few filthy rags almost alive with vermin, their bodies rotting with distemper and covered with itch, scorbutic and venereal ulcers."[65]

Wesley occasionally visited the jails in Oxford, London, Bristol, and elsewhere. He sometimes preached, read the Bible, gave communion, prayed with the prisoners, provided food and clothing, and saw prisoners find forgiveness in Jesus Christ. In fact, the first person to which he records having offered salvation by faith alone was an Oxford prisoner named Clifford who was under the sentence of death.[66] In 1753, he visited Marshalsea Prison. He called the prison "a nursery of all manner of wickedness. Oh shame to man that there should be such a place, such a picture of hell upon earth!" He declaimed it a shame that a country where Christianity had been established should need any prison at all.[67]

In 1759, the British were holding eleven hundred French prisoners in Knowle, just a mile from Bristol. John Wesley went to see them. He was much affected by the scandalous lack of humane treatment. He preached that evening on, "Thou shalt not oppress a stranger." He got immediate contributions in which cloth was purchased and clothing made. These were distributed to the most needy prisoners. Though the context is unclear, the inference from Wesley's journal is that his call initiated the Corporation of Bristol and others from across the kingdom to send bedding and other necessities of life to the prisoners.[68]

Other Methodists who made visiting the prison a regular ministry modeled Wesley's example. Sarah Peters became a faithful prison visitor. John Wesley said it was her "peculiar gift, and her continual care, to seek and save that which was lost."[69] She went continually to Newgate, sometimes alone, to visit all that were condemned to death in their cells. She exhorted from Scripture, prayed with them and found increasing thirst for God.

A wayward Methodist named John Lancaster had stolen property from City Road Chapel. He was arrested, tried, and condemned to death. Believing he did not deserve death, Sarah sought a pardon for him, to no avail. She was undeterred by a severe outbreak of dangerous, contagious fever in London's Newgate prison. Just a few days before John Lancaster's hanging, she saw a change in him. In the meantime, she became gravely ill—probably jail fever—and died just ten days later.[70] One sees in Sarah Peters and her mentor John Wesley the twinning of personal and social concern for both prisoners' bodies and souls.

In his vigorous commitment to experiential, personal knowledge of Jesus Christ and the love of God and neighbor, Wesley believed that the restoration of the image of God in the believer encompassed bringing the passions and intellect into conformity to Christ. He took at keen interest in education, but not just any education would do. Plato and Socrates' only goal in educating was teaching people how to think and judge and act accordingly. For Wesley, Christian education's only goal was to teach how to think and judge and act according to the rule of Christianity. It helped people discover the false judgments of the mind and subdue every wrong passion.[71]

In promoting the need for educating the Christian mind and will, Wesley gave incentive for education to the laboring class. The inspiration to know the mind of Christ in Holy Scripture gave motivation to read.[72] In Britain, though most males of the middling class could read, just more than half of the male laboring population was literate.[73] Early Methodist preachers like ironworker Francis Asbury came mainly from trades. Some said they did not like to read, or reading the Bible was all the reading they needed to do. Wesley countered them by saying, "Reading Christians will be knowing Christians." One needed to read beyond the Bible to avoid being dull. So, he provided the preaching houses with a fifty-volume library called The Christian Library. Augmenting the reading of

Scripture, The Christian Library contained the best works of divinity simplified for his uneducated followers.

Wesley also established and oversaw four Kingswood schools for boys and girls; it was a lifetime labor of love. He originally designed the schools for the general Christian public; they were to be Christian schools free of the dubious educational methods, religious, and moral atmosphere of the "great schools." The school was designed to "train up children . . . in every branch of useful learning" with hopes they would be fit with the qualifications for the work of ministry. He sought to form the children's minds and wills, through God's help, to wisdom and holiness.[74] The concern for educating young minds to wisdom and holiness along the Kingswood model was emulated by the American Methodists. On the cusp of the Christmas Conference of 1784, which formed the Methodist Episcopal Church, a project for a Methodist college was already being broached and materials were to be collected.[75] Methodist education began with Cokesbury in Maryland, with proposals following for others schools in Georgia, North Carolina, and Kentucky.[76] Educating people for the need for Christian education was itself a hurdle. Asbury lamented that "people, in general, care too little for the education of their children."[77] Methodist concern for bringing wills and minds into conformity to Christ through Christian education was as real as the legacy of many of our colleges and national universities such as Southern California, Syracuse, Emory, and Duke.

Love for others who were the work of the Creator's hands and the purchase of the Son's blood was motivation enough for John Wesley to commend liberty for all and to condemn black slavery.[78] Black slavery was a national scourge which Wesley spoke against locally and as a prominent national leader. Likewise, American Methodist leaders Thomas Coke and Francis Asbury echoed his sentiment in appealing for action against slavery in America.

Wesley encountered slavery as a missionary in Georgia. He firmly supported the administrator James Oglethorpe and the Georgia colony trustees in their policy to outlaw the slave trade.[79] Wesley also provided some of the slaves with Christian instruction.[80]

During the eighteenth century, the slave trade was turning handsome profits. The triangle of England, West Africa, and the West

Indies and America was thriving off of it. Ships sailed from Liverpool and Bristol (up to thirty thousand slaves a year) to West Africa to capture the Africans. They were then transported to the Caribbean and America to work the sugar and cotton plantations. Sugar and cotton were sold in return.

In 1774, John Wesley wrote a powerful tract against slavery. He called slavery a detestable business procured by a deliberate series of more complicated villainy (of fraud, robbery, and murder) than was ever practiced either by Mahometans or Pagans. Liberty was the right of every human person who breathes the air. No human law can deprive one of this right.[81]

To a Bristol "New Room" full of high and low, rich and poor, he preached on slavery. The next day was set apart for fasting and prayer "that God would remember those poor outcasts of men."[82] Moved by reading the life of the black slave Gustavus Vassa, Wesley, in what was likely his last letter, wrote encouragement to House of Commons representative William Wilberforce in his campaign to eradicate slavery in England. He urged him to, "Go on, in the name of God and in the power of His might, till even American slavery (the vilest that ever saw the sun) shall vanish away before it."[83]

American Methodists were in lockstep with their English brethren. They opposed slavery through conference action and preaching, and by appeal to government leaders. In 1780, a conference measure was passed to require preachers holding slaves to promise to set them free. Slavery was condemned as against the laws of God, humankind, and nature. This was reiterated in the conference of 1783.[84] The 1784 conference stated that members who continued to hold slaves after having been warned against it would be expelled.[85] In 1785, the conference drafted a petition to the General Assembly of North Carolina to encourage persons to emancipate their slaves. Asbury visited with the governor and received his backing.[86]

Methodist preachers, with few exceptions, were emancipationists and preached courageously against slavery. They, including Thomas Coke, were threatened, even mobbed, for their stance. Coke and Asbury made an appointment with President George Washington to appeal to him to oppose slavery. After dining with the President at Mt. Vernon, they met with him in private to present a petition for the emancipation of blacks. Agreeing with their sentiments but refusing to sign it, he said he would support an assembly measure to that effect.[87] Notwithstanding these strongly held views, and in what is now seen as a tragic move, Asbury, trying to hold the conference together, compromised with slavery proponents that same year allowing the conference to suspend its former rules against slavery.[88]

John Wesley and the Methodists are exemplary in Christian history as authentic proponents of both evangelical faith and social love, justification by faith and good works, inward and outward religion, the personal and the social. Through their own personal experience of the love of God and the love of humankind in justification and sanctification, they offered to any who would receive the possibility of full redemption from ills of soul and body. Holding together both personal pardon and social love, the higher goal of the salvation of souls was the deepest motivation for social mercies of bodies.

Appendix C

The New Testament and the Priority of the Gospel Proclamation

Rev. Christopher T. Bounds, PhD

The New Testament bears repeated, strong witness to the sinfulness of humankind and the salvation provided for us through the atoning death of Jesus Christ. Salvation comes to the individual by faith through the hearing of the Gospel and a personal response to it. Wesleyan and New Testament scholar Dr. Christopher M. Bounds has written about the New Testament and the priority of Gospel proclamation.

In historic Protestant articles of religion, confessions of faith, and catechetical questions on the Church, the preaching of the pure Word of God is identified as the first mark of the Church. While other marks are inevitably mentioned, such as the due administration of the sacraments and the community rightly ordered, priority is given to proclamation.[1] The purpose is not to minimize the importance of sacraments or church discipline, both of which are necessary for the Church to be the Church, but to recognize the Church as the community distinguished principally by the preaching of the Gospel. From a Protestant perspective, preaching is the primary channel through which the Holy Spirit works to bring the Church into being and through which its existence is sustained.

The priority of proclamation is one of the fundamental differences Protestantism has with other forms of Christianity. While the Roman Catholic Church and the Eastern Orthodox Church also recognize preaching, sacraments, and order as distinguishing marks of the

Church, they order them differently in their respective understandings. The Roman Catholic Church emphasizes the "community rightly ordered." The Church is primarily distinguished by its appointed bishop, who is in an ordered relationship with the papacy in Rome. Without a bishop connecting a local congregation to the Pope, without a local church being properly related to the larger Church in Rome, the status of the local church as a part of the true Church is called into question. The Eastern Orthodox Church, on the other hand, focuses on the sacraments, particularly the celebration of the Eucharist, as the defining mark. The sacraments are the primary means of God's grace, calling the Church into being and sustaining its existence. Without the sacraments, there is no Church of Jesus Christ.[2]

Specifically, The United Methodist Church, in its Article of Religion and Confession of Faith on the Church, places preaching the pure Word of God as the first mark of the true Church. The Article of Religion, which comes directly from the Anglican tradition, states, "The visible Church of Christ is a congregation of faithful men in which the pure Word of God is preached . . ." and the Confession of Faith, which comes from the Evangelical United Brethren denomination, declares the church to be "the redemptive fellowship in which the Word of God is preached. . . ."[3] While each recognizes the importance of sacrament and ecclesial discipline, priority is given to proclamation.

This primacy of proclamation found in Protestantism, and more particularly in The United Methodist Church's doctrinal standards, is grounded in the clear teaching of the New Testament. There is no Church of Jesus Christ and there is no mission of the Church apart from the preaching of the pure word of God. Proclamation cannot be divorced from the Church's nature and mission. The Word of God brings the Church into existence, sustains the Church, and forms the primary mission of the Church in the world. In order to see this more clearly, we will examine the New Testament teaching on proclamation. To begin, we will see the priority and place of preaching in the ministry of Jesus; then, we will examine the purpose of proclamation in the New Testament Church and conclude with application to our contemporary context in The United Methodist Church.

THE PRIORITY AND PURPOSE OF PROCLAMATION IN THE MINISTRY OF JESUS

As described in the Gospel texts, the earthly ministry of Jesus is defined by activity. Christ healed, drove out demons, performed miracles, confronted injustice, appointed disciples, forgave sins, exercised authority over the law, and showed compassion on the needy. Jesus described proclamation of the Kingdom of God as His primary task.

At the beginning of His ministry Jesus declared, "Let us go somewhere else—to the nearby villages—so I can preach there also. That is why I have come" (Mark 1:38).[4] In His home synagogue in Nazareth, Jesus appropriated the words of Isaiah to define His ministry as a call to "proclaim good news to the poor . . . proclaim freedom for prisoners . . . and proclaim the year of the Lord's favor" (Luke 4:18–19). This is corroborated by Matthew, who begins his description of Jesus' public ministry with the declaration, "From that time on Jesus began to preach, 'Repent, for the kingdom of heaven is near'" (Matt. 4:17). As such, Jesus' miracles are portrayed in the Gospels as powerful signs of the Kingdom He proclaimed. His healings and exorcisms are recognized as works of compassion, the firstfruits of the presence of the Kingdom of God he proclaimed in the world. The Gospel writers place the whole body of Jesus' public ministry within the larger context of and in relationship to Jesus' proclamation of the Kingdom of God.

While the Gospels portray Jesus' primary mission in public ministry as proclamation, they make clear that Jesus himself is the key to the Kingdom. There is no Kingdom of God apart from Jesus Christ. Through his presence, his ministry and particularly his preaching, Christ initiates and mediates the Kingdom of God (Matt. 12:28, Luke 11:20, 17:20–21).

The intimate relationship between Christ and the Kingdom he proclaimed is manifested in multiple ways throughout the Gospels. Implicitly, this is seen in the authority exercised by Jesus in the establishment of the Kingdom. In every account of the Kingdom of God breaking into the present order, in healings, exorcisms, and the declaration of the forgiveness of sins, Jesus worked by his own authority, in his own name, not in the name of another (Matt. 8:28–34; Mark 2:1–12; Luke 7:47–49, 15:1–2). In his preaching on the Kingdom, Jesus declared, "I say to you," and did not use the more traditional prophetic utterance, "thus says the Lord" (Matt. 5:21–44). Furthermore, He exercised authority over the written law by setting aside its stipulations on such matters as retribution, divorce, food, and the Sabbath (Matt. 5:21–48; Mark 2:23–28, 3:1–5, 7:15, 19). Most glaringly, He preached a new relationship with God that would be brought about through His own life, a new relationship that would put aside the Temple in Jerusalem, the central place of Jewish religious life (Mark 11:15–17, 27–33).[5]

Explicitly, the relationship between Christ and the Kingdom He proclaimed is seen in His definitive declarations, "I am the way, the truth, and the life. No one comes to the Father except through me" (John 14:6), and "I am the bread of life. No one who comes to me will ever go hungry. And no one who believes in me will ever be thirsty" (John 6:35). Jesus' testimony of Himself was an essential part of His proclamation of the Kingdom.

Jesus spoke of the Kingdom as already "here" through His presence, His ministry, and His preaching, as well as to come in the future. His proclamation of the Kingdom had both a "now" and "not yet" aspect to it (Matt. 4:17, 6:10; Mark 1:15, 9:1; Luke 11:2). In the present, He saw His ministry and proclamation as the climax of God's present purposes for Israel and the means through which the reign of God in the world was initiated. In the future, He saw Himself as being the central authority in bringing others into the final consummation of the kingdom at the end of time. He taught that a person's place in the future kingdom was directly related to that individual's relationship and standing with Jesus in the present life (Matt. 10:32–33, 12:32; Luke 12:8–9).

In summary, Jesus primarily saw the task of His public ministry as proclamation of the Kingdom of God. All His other work was to illustrate and mediate the Kingdom He proclaimed. This was the purpose of His preaching. His proclamation was the primary means by which the Kingdom was inaugurated in the world, the means through which the reign of God broke into human existence, and how people experienced signs of the kingdom. However, Jesus was not simply a messenger, but was

Himself the key to the Kingdom of God in the present life and in the future age to come.

The Gospels make clear that there is no experience of the Kingdom apart from Jesus' work of proclamation and the authority Jesus himself exercised in God's reign.

THE PRIORITY AND PURPOSE OF PROCLAMA- TION IN THE NEW TESTAMENT CHURCH

The priority of proclamation in Jesus' ministry is transferred to His disciples as well. Luke states in his Gospel that during Christ's public ministry, Jesus appointed seventy-two people to go two by two into the surrounding villages to proclaim that the "Kingdom of God is near" (Luke 10:9). He promised them that when they would preach to the crowds, He would speak through their words (Luke 10:16). In a similar event in Matthew, Jesus' commissions the twelve apostles to go and preach the message that the "Kingdom of heaven is near" (10:7). While Jesus gave His disciples authority to heal sicknesses and cast out demons, this was within the larger context of preaching His message (10:1–8), a message not intended for a select few, but one meant for the entire world (10:26–27).

This priority did not change after Christ's death and resurrection. Before his assumption into heaven, Jesus commanded his followers to go into all the world and make disciples (Matt. 28:19). After the Holy Spirit was given to the disciples on the day of Pentecost, they were empowered to preach in Jerusalem and the church was formed. The Gospel was then proclaimed in Judea and Samaria, where it was received with great joy (Acts 8:8). The Gospel message was then preached in Antioch to the Gentiles and the "Lord's power was with them" (Acts 11:19). In Antioch, Paul and Barnabas were commissioned to go and proclaim the Gospel in the Roman world, preaching first to the Jews and then the Gentiles (Acts 13:2–3). The Book of Acts concludes with Paul arriving in Rome, with the declaration that Paul "proclaimed the Kingdom of God and taught about the Lord Jesus Christ—with all boldness and without hindrance," and with the anticipation that the Gospel of Jesus Christ would be proclaimed to the uttermost parts of the earth

(28:31). While there were threats to the priority of preaching, as in the dispute of the daily distribution of food to the widows (6:1–3) and the controversy surrounding the incorporation of the Gentiles into the Church (10:9–48; 15:1–29), the apostles were able to maintain their focus and continued their proclamation of the "word of God" (6:3; 15:35).

In a similar way, just as Jesus' proclamation of the Kingdom of God was a means through which the Kingdom broke into human existence, the preaching of the Gospel by the disciples became a means by which the salvific effects of Christ's life, death, and resurrection were experienced by the New Testament Church, a means by which the Kingdom of God broke into human existence. The purpose of proclamation by the disciples was made clear by Christ. In the same way, Christ's life, death, and resurrection was necessary to bring about the redemption of humanity, so the proclamation of the Gospel is also necessary to bring about God's saving plan for humanity. After His resurrection, Jesus told His disciples that this plan was a fulfillment of Scriptures, "This is what is written: the messiah will suffer and rise from the dead on the third day, and repentance for the forgiveness of sins will be preached in his name to all nations. . . ." (Luke 24:46–47).

It is not enough that Christ lived, died, and was raised from the dead. These facts must be proclaimed in order that they may become a saving reality for individuals. Hence, the apostle Paul spoke not only about the cross of Christ, but also about the message of the cross as the power of God to save (1 Cor. 1:18); he spoke not only about people being reconciled to God through Christ, but about the power of the words of reconciliation to bring about reconciliation to God (2 Cor. 5:19). Again, the work of Jesus and the proclamation of that work by the disciples make possible the work of salvation and the experience of the Kingdom of God.

Perhaps this is made most clear by Paul in the book of Romans. Paul teaches that everyone that believes in Jesus Christ (10:9) and calls upon his name will be saved (10:13). Paul then asks the question, "How, then can they call on the one they have not believed in? And how can they believe in the one of whom they have not heard? And how can they hear without someone preaching to them? And how can anyone preach unless they are sent?" (10:14–15). He goes on to clarify that faith that brings about salvation is a gift from God that comes from hearing the word of God (10:17).

Preaching the word of God is the means by which God works in humanity to bring faith in Jesus Christ. Without the preaching of the Gospel, what Christ accomplished through his death and resurrection cannot be brought about in human hearts and lives. The Kingdom as proclaimed and inaugurated by Christ cannot be realized apart from the proclamation of the Gospel, apart from the preaching of the word of God.

In summary, the priority given to preaching in Jesus' public ministry is transferred to his disciples. This is seen in the disciples' work of proclamation before and after the resurrection of Christ. While the life, death, and resurrection of Christ accomplished the objective work of salvation, the preaching of the Gospel is what God uses to subjectively make it possible in people's lives. This is the purpose of Christian proclamation. Through preaching of the word of God, Christ works through the disciples' proclamation to establish the kingdom of God here on earth and prepare humanity for the consummation of that Kingdom in the age to come. Just as there is no Kingdom apart from Jesus Christ, there is no Kingdom without the proclamation of the Gospel. Proclamation makes possible Christian faith in Christ and actualizes the salvific work of Christ in the present experience of humanity. Hence, Christ commissions the apostles to preach, with proclamation as the clearly stated priority in the New Testament Church.[6]

RELEVANCE TO THE CONTEMPORARY UNITED METHODIST CHURCH

In regard to the present state of The United Methodist Church and the denomination's social witness, three related points can be made. First, in the mission and ministry of the denomination, proclamation of the Gospel must remain central, as demonstrated in the ministry of Jesus, the early New Testament Church, and encapsulated in Protestantism's historic articles of religion and confessions of faith. The Kingdom of God is experienced and advanced through the proclamation of the Gospel. Where the message of Jesus is preached, where the word of God is proclaimed, the Kingdom in its life-transforming reign becomes possible.

God's reign, as established through Jesus, does not happen apart from Christian proclamation. If The United Methodist Church wants to transform human societies and cultures, then the Church must not forsake or minimize the priority of preaching the pure word of God.

Proclamation of the pure word of God has this power because it is one of the primary means or channels of God's grace in the world. In any discussion of God's grace, which may be defined simply as the unmerited work of God for humanity, in humanity, and through humanity, the question must be asked, "How does God communicate His grace to people? How does God work in people?" The Scriptures reveal that God communicates His grace through appointed channels or means. While recognizing other means of grace, other channels through which God works, the New Testament makes clear that divine grace is communicated first and foremost through the preaching of the Word of God.

Second, and intimately related to the first point, the content of the proclamation must center on the life, death, resurrection, and exaltation of Christ. Jesus Christ must be the Word of God proclaimed. He is the key to the present experience of the reign of God in human life and the future as well. As such, The United Methodist Church's social witness must be marked by an unapologetic and vocal witness to the Lordship of Jesus Christ. He must be the primary content of the Gospel proclaimed. Proclamation without focus on Christ's salvific life is powerless to bring about true, life-transforming change in human lives. Where Jesus Christ is not preached, then there can be no experience of the power of salvation.

While The United Methodist Church has an admirable history of teachings on social justice, advocacy for disenfranchised groups through governmental legislation, and empathetic identification with the least and the last of human society, these actions are weakened and incomplete apart from proclamation centering on the salvific life of Christ.

Finally, as has already been stated, the word of God, the Gospel of Jesus Christ, is meant for the entire world. Jesus intended the Gospel to go to every nation and every culture, to the whole world and not just a part. Unfortunately, The United Methodist Church has been timid and reluctant to preach the Gospel in other cultures where Christianity is not already present. There has been a tendency to see other world religions as equally valid, as another "word of God," on par with the Gospel. To refuse or neglect taking the Gospel of Jesus Christ into every culture, however, is to deny them access to grace that can bring true personal and social transformation. The United Methodist Church must recommit to world evangelism in obedience to the command of Christ and in true love for those who have not had access to the transforming power of Christ's life, death, resurrection, and exaltation, made available through proclamation.

It is not by accident that Protestantism has emphasized the priority of Gospel proclamation in historic doctrinal standards. This emphasis is grounded in the public ministry of Jesus, the commission given by Christ to his disciples, and in the practice of the early Church. Proclamation is the primary means by which the Kingdom of God is advanced in the world. Christ works through the Church's proclamation to create in people's lives the reality described in it.

The United Methodist Church, in its mission and ministry and in the recovery of its social witness, must once again commit itself to the task of preaching the Word of God, of proclaiming the Gospel. While proclamation is not the only means by which God's redeeming and transforming grace is made available in the world, it is central. True social change, true inculcation of the Kingdom of God cannot happen apart from sharing the Gospel. In this regard, the church must recover what is clearly stated and indicated in its doctrine and summarized in its doctrinal standards.

NOTES

Preface

1. Kenneth Cain Kinghorn, *John Wesley on Christian Beliefs: The Standard Sermons in Modern English* (Nashville: Abingdon Press, 2002), vol. 1, 39.

2. Ibid., 42.

3. Ibid., 55.

Chapter 1

1. Homilies have reference to written sermons or lectures of the Church of England.

2. Henry Carter, *The Methodist Heritage* (Nashville: Abingdon Press, 1951), 16.

3. Ibid., 27.

4. Ibid., 26.

5. Ibid., 28.

6. Ibid., 26. The hymn of five stanzas was titled "The Wesleys' Conversion Hymn. Whitsuntide, 1728" in the *Methodist Hymnbook. The United Methodist Hymnal* places this hymn on page 342, offering six verses and stating that there were originally eight verses to the hymn.

7. Kenneth Cain Kinghorn, *John Wesley on Christian Beliefs: The Standard Sermons in Modern English* (Nashville: Abingdon Press, 2002), vol. 1, 1–20, 30.

8. Carter, *The Methodist Heritage*, 14.

9. Ibid., 16–17.

10. Ibid., 46–48.

11. John Wesley, "Plain Account of Christian Perfection," *The Works of John Wesley*, ed. Thomas Jackson (Grand Rapids: Baker, 1986), vol. 11, para. 5.

12. Carter, *The Methodist Heritage*, 38–39, 45.

13. Ibid., 43.

14. Ibid., 25.

15. Ibid., 26–27.

16. Ibid., 28.

17. From Charles Wesley's correspondence, in Frank Baker, *Charles Wesley As Revealed by His Letters* (London: Epworth Press, 1948), n.p.

18. H. O. "Tom" Thomas Jr., "The Historical Wesleyan Witness," (unpublished essay, 2007), 12.

19. Manfred Marquardt, *John Wesley's Social Ethics: Praxis and Principles*, trans. John E. Steely and W. Stephen Gunter (Nashville: Abingdon Press, 1992), 12.

20. John Wesley, "On Visiting the Sick," *Works III*, Jackson edition, vol. 12, sermon 98, 123.

21. Marquardt, *John Wesley's Social Ethics*, 32.

22. Albert C. Outler and Richard P. Heitzenrater, eds., *John Wesley Sermons: An Anthology* (Nashville: Abingdon Press), 347.

23. Richard P. Heitzenrater, ed. *The Poor and the People called Methodist* (Nashville: Kingswood Books/Abingdon Press, 2002), 36.

24. Herbert Schlossberg, "How Great Awakenings Happen," *First Things*, (October 2000), 48.

25. Ibid., 49.

26. Ibid.

Chapter 2

1. Kinghorn, *John Wesley on Christian Beliefs: The Standard Sermons in Modern English* (Nashville: Abingdon Press, 2002), 39.

2. Ibid., 42.

3. Ibid., 55.

4. Wesley, *Works*, Jackson, 14, 321.

5. Ibid., 320.

6. H. O. "Tom" Thomas Jr., *The Historical Wesleyan Witness* (unpublished essay, 2007), 5.

7. Carl F. H. Henry, *A Plea for Evangelical Demonstration* (Grand Rapids: Baker Book House, 1971), 107.

8. Thomas, "The Historical Wesleyan Witness," 2.

9. William Temple, "Christianity and the Social Order," in *Devotional Classics*, ed. Richard Foster and James Bryan Smith (San Francisco: Harper San Francisco, 1993), 252.

10. National Association of Evangelicals, *For the Health of the Nation: An Evangelical Call to Civic Responsibility*, (Washington, D.C.: National Association of Evangelicals, 2004), 1–3.

11. Ronald J. Sider and Diane Knippers, *Toward An Evangelical Public Policy* (Grand Rapids: Baker Books, 2005), 9–10.

12. Christopher T. Bounds, "The New Testament and the Priority of Gospel Proclamation" (unpublished essay, 2007), 4–5.

13. Dallas Willard, *The Great Omission* (San Francisco: Harper, 1998), 11.

14. Ibid., 11–12.

15. Alan Richardson and John Bowden, eds., "Culture," in *The Westminster Dictionary of Christian Theology* (Philadelphia: The Westminster Press, 1983).

16. Bounds, "The New Testament," 6.

Chapter 3

1. John Wesley, "Of the Gradual Improvement of Natural Philosophy," in *The Works of John Wesley*, ed. Thomas Jackson (Grand Rapids: Baker, 1986), vol. 13, 487.

2. Kenneth Cain Kinghorn, *John Wesley on Christian Beliefs: The Standard Sermons in Modern English* (Nashville: Abingdon Press, 2002),vol. 1, 1–20, 30 .

3. Timothy L. Smith, *Revivalism and Social Reform* (Baltimore: The Johns Hopkins University Press, 1980), 219.

4. Roger Finke and Rodney Starke, *The Churching of America 1776–2005* (New Brunswick, NJ: Rutgers University Press, 2005), 175.

5. See Smith, *Revivalism and Social Reform*, and Melvin Dieter, *The 19th Century Holiness Movement* (Kansas City, MO: Beacon Hill Press, 1998) for additional information on the Holiness Movement.

6. Dr. Elaine Heath, "What Would Phoebe Do?" (unpublished essay, 2007), 2.

7. Donald W. Dayton, *Discovering an Evangelical Heritage* (New York: Harper and Row, 1976), 88–89.

8. Ibid., 95. Dayton states, "It was perhaps Frances Willard rather than the more radical feminists who made suffrage more palatable to the masses."

9. Ibid., 94.

10. Ibid., 96.

11. Ibid., 112.

12. Ibid., 113.

13. Ibid., 116.

14. Ibid., 117.

15. Smith, *Revivalism and Social Reform*, 167, 176.

16. Stephen L. Carter, *God's Name in Vain* (New York: Basic Books, 2000), 104.

17. Marvin Olasky, "Capital Shakeup," *World* (May 20, 2006): 48.

18. Michael Novak, "Controversial Engagements," *First Things* (April 1999): 27.

19. James V. Heidinger II, *United Methodist Renewal: What Will It Take?* (Wilmore, KY: Bristol Books, 1988), 27.

20. A study released in September 2005 by Ellison Research showed a continued disparity between the political and social beliefs of both clergy and people in the pews. The study concluded, "Among Methodist laity, just 12 percent are politically liberal, while the figure is 35 percent among Methodist clergy."

21. Heidinger, *United Methodist Renewal*, 33–34.

22. Herbert Welch, "The Church and Social Service," *Methodist Review* XC (Sept.–Oct. 1908): 714.

23. Frances J. McConnell, *Christian Citizenship* (New York: The Methodist Book Concern, 1922), 7.

24. Ibid., 39.

25. Mark A. Noll, *The Scandal of the Evangelical Mind* (Grand Rapids: William B. Eerdmans Publishing Company, 1994), 119.

26. Ibid., 115.

27. John C. Green, "Seeking a Place," in *Toward An Evangelical Public Policy* (Grand Rapids: Baker Books 2005), 26–27.

28. Robert E. Chiles, *Theological Transition in American Methodism: 1790–1935* (Lanham: University Press of America, Inc., 1983), 26.

29. Albert C. Outler and Richard P. Heitzenrater, eds., "Catholic Spirit," in *John Wesley's Sermons: An Anthology* (Nashville: Abingdon Press, 1991), 307.

30. Chiles, *Theological Transition*, 27.

Chapter 4

1. Kenneth Cain Kinghorn, *John Wesley on The Sermon on the Mount* (Nashville: Abingdon Press, 2002), 12.

2. Albert Outler, "Justification by Faith," *John Wesley's Sermons: An Anthology* (Nashville: Abingdon Press, 1991), (III.5), 1:192–93.

3. Outler, "On Working Out Our Own Salvation" (III, 7), 3:208

4. Kinghorn, *The Sermon on the Mount*, 16.

5. Outler, "Sermon on the Mount," Discourse 5 (II,3), 1:554

6. Kinghorn, *The Sermon on the Mount*, 19.

7. Ibid., 21.

8. Outler, "Self-Denial," (I, 1), 2:240.

9. Kinghorn, *The Sermon on the Mount*, 27.

10. Dallas Willard, *The Divine Conspiracy* (San Francisco: Harper, 1998), 50.

11. Ibid., 51n15: "For an example, see James F. Findlay, *Church People in the Struggle: The National Council of Churches and the Black Freedom Movement, 1950–1970* (New York: Oxford University Press, 1994)."

12. The "theological left" may also be termed the "religious left" or "Christian left." Wikipedia states, "The 'Religious Left' is a term used to describe those who hold strong religious beliefs and share left-wing ideals. . . . As with any division into left-wing and right-wing, a label is always an approximation . . . which may or may not be held by different Christian movements and individuals. . . . The most common religious viewpoint which might be described as 'left wing' is social justice, or care for the poor. Supporters of this might encourage universal health care, generous welfare, subsidized education, foreign aid, and government subsidized schemes for improving the conditions for the disadvantaged." See http://en.wikipedia.org/wiki/Christian_left. In the usage in this paper, "theological left" would also identify those who hold a liberal view of the Gospel, questioning many of the basic tenants of the Christian faith such as the virgin birth, the need for atoning the death of Christ, the original sin, the bodily resurrection of Christ and the imminent return of Christ to the earth. On matters of human sexuality, those of a liberal

theological persuasion would be most likely to consider the practice of homosexuality acceptable.

13. Richard John Neuhaus, "Feminism and Feminism," *First Things* (June/July 1992): 66–67. Available on the Web at www.firstthings.com.

14. Mary A. Kassian, *The Feminist Gospel* (Wheaton, IL: Crossway, 1992), 54.

15. Willard, *The Divine Conspiracy*, 50. For a discussion of how the NCC laid the foundation for the Gospel to be seen in terms of social activism, see Findlay, *Church People in the Struggle: The National Council of Churches and the Black Freedom Movement* (New York: Oxford University Press, 1994.)

16. For a discussion of the early WCC commitment to liberation theology, see Raymond C. Hundley, *Radical Liberation Theology: An Evangelical Response* (Wilmore, KY: Bristol Books, 1984), 77–82. More recent expressions of this continued commitment can be found at ww.wcc-coe.org.

17. This is easy to see when considering the Nazi ideology that led the world into war in the 1940s and exterminated millions of Jews. It is equally easy to see when we consider that Marxist ideology, as it was applied in the Soviet Union, led to the deaths of millions of innocent people and the persecution of countless others in an attempt to bring justice to the oppressed people of Russia and eastern Europe. But, it is not always easy to distinguish

between mere ideologies (visionary theorizing) and biblical principles.

18. Richard John Neuhaus, "The Gods of Left and Right," *First Things* (March 1999): 63.

19. Thomas C. Oden, *Turning Around The Mainline* (Grand Rapids: Baker Books, 2006), 23.

20. Ibid., 69.

Chapter 5

1. John Wesley "Thoughts upon Methodism," in *The Works of John Wesley*, ed. Thomas Jackson (London: Wesleyan Methodist Book Room, 1872), reprinted by Baker Book House, 1978, 13, 259.

2. Kenneth Cain Kinghorn, *John Wesley on Christian Beliefs: The Standard Sermons in Modern English* (Nashville: Abingdon Press, 2002), 20.

3. Riley B. Case, *Evangelical & Methodist: A Popular History* (Nashville: Abingdon Press, 2004), 13.

4. Henry Carter, *The Methodist Heritage* (Nashville: Abingdon Press, 1951), 144.

5. Ibid.

6. Ibid.

7. Ibid., 145.

8. Ibid., 150–51.

9. Ibid., 143.

10. Kenneth Cain Kinghorn, *The Heritage of American Methodism* (Nashville: Abingdon Press, 1999), 51.

11. Ibid., 59.

12. Roger Finke and Rodney Stark, *The Churching of America 1776–2005* (New Brunswick, NJ: Rutgers University Press, 2005), 79. This quote is taken from T. Scott Miyakawa, *Protestants and Pioneers* (Chicago: University of Chicago Press, 1964), 90–91.

13. Ibid., 84.

14. Ibid., 100–101.

15. Ibid., 103. The most famous black preacher was the Methodist itinerant Harry Hosier, known as Black Harry. He often traveled and preached with the Methodist bishops in the 1780s and 1790s and the crowd sizes he drew frequently surpassed those of the bishops. Although he was typically scheduled to preach for the Blacks, Bishop Coke soon learned that the "whites always stay near to hear him."

16. Ibid., 82.

17. Ibid., 168.

18. Finke and Stark, *The Churching of America*, 206. Quotes are taken from James Madison, "Reformers and the Rural Church, 1900-1950." *Journal of American History* 73: 645-668.

19. Richard B. Wilke, *And Are We Yet Alive?* (Nashville: Abingdon Press, 1986), 9.

20. William H. Willimon and Robert Leroy Wilson, *Rekindling the Flame* (Nashville: Abingdon Press, 1987), 11–12. Willimon and Wilson note that Methodist statistics are from the annual editions of the General Minutes of the Annual Conferences of The United Methodist Church (Evanston, IL: Council on Finance and Administration, 968–1985). Rates of change have been computed by the authors.

21. GFCA Web site, April 2007, www.gcfa.org.

22. Finke and Stark, *The Churching of America*, 249.

23. Ibid., 248.

24. Willimon and Wilson, *Rekindling the Flame*, 26.

25. Ibid., 31.

26. John Wesley, *The Bicentennial Edition of the Works of John Wesley*, ed. Frank Baker, 34 vols. (Nashville: Abingdon Press, 1984), 3, 393.

27. Leicester Longden, Assoc. Professor of Evangelism and Discipleship, University of Dubuque Theological Seminary, "The Recovery, Reform, and Renewal of Membership Practices," 4. See www.gbhem.org/asp/resourceLibrary .asp. This paper was prepared for a Theological Consultation on Membership, Ecclesiology, and Leadership convened by the General Board of Higher Education and Ministry on February 15–16, 2007.

28. Richard J. Neuhaus, *The Naked Public Square* (Grand Rapids: William B. Eerdmans Publishing Co., 1986), 125.

29. E-mail from RENEW prayer team member, January 2007.

30. Willimon and Wilson, *Rekindling the Flame*, 30.

31. Thomas O. Oden, *Turning Around the Mainline* (Grand Rapids: Baker Books, 2006), 112.

32. Ibid., 69.

33. Stephen L. Carter, *God's Name in Vain* (New York: Basic Books, 2000), 192.

34. archives.umc.org/interior.asp?ptid= 1&mid=4311-36k

35. National Association of Evangelicals, *For the Health of a Nation: An Evangelical Call to Civic Responsibility*, (Washington, D.C.: National Association of Evangelicals, 2004): 3–4.

Chapter 6

1. Albert Outler, *John Wesley* (Oxford: Oxford University Press, 1964), 173. See Steve Harper, *John Wesley's Message for Today* (Grand Rapids: Francis Asbury Press, 1983), 120.

2. Henry Carter, *The Methodist Heritage* (Nashville: Abingdon Press, 1951), 154. citing Wesley's *Journal*, VII. 422

3. Harper, *John Wesley's Message for Today* (Grand Rapids: Zondervan Publishing House, 1983), 117.

4. Carter, *The Methodist Heritage*, 52.

5. J. Wesley Bready, *England: Before and After Wesley* (London: Hodder and Stoughton, 1983), 177, in James V. Heidinger II, *United Methodist Renewal: What Will It Take?* (Wilmore, KY: Bristol Books, 1988), 20.

6. Harper, *John Wesley's Message for Today*, 20.

7. John Wesley, "Causes for the Inefficacy of Christianity," in *The Works of John Wesley*, ed. Thomas Jackson (Grand Rapids: Baker, 1986), 7: 281–283.

8. Harper, *John Wesley's Message for Today*, 21.

9. William J. Abraham, *Waking from Doctrinal Amnesia* (Nashville: Abingdon Press, 1995), 81–85.

10. Janice Shaw Crouse, *Gaining Ground: A Profile of American Women in the Twentieth Century* (Washington, DC: Beverly LaHaye Institute, 2000), 12, 29.

11. Bruce Bartlett, National Center for Policy Analysis report, May 27, 2002. www. ncpa.org.

12. Leon R. Kass, "Regarding Daughters and Sister: The Rape of Dinah," in *The Essential Neo-Conservative Reader*, ed. Mark Gerson, (Reading, MA: Addison-Wesley Publishing Co., 1996), 354–55.

13. Crouse, *Gaining Ground*, 11.

14. Bradford W. Wilcox, "The Facts of Life and Marriage; Social Science and the Vindication of Christian Moral Teaching," in *Touchstone*, (January/February 2005): vol. 18, 1, 44. Available at www.touchstonemag.com/archives/article.php?id=18-01-038-f.

15. Sarah McLanahan and Gary Sandefur, *Growing Up With a Single Parent* (Boston: Harvard University Press, 1994), n.p.

16. Wilcox, "The Facts of Life," 39, 43.

17. Ibid., 43.

18. Ibid.

19. A study conducted by the Barna Research Group from interviews with 3,854 adults from forty-eight states found that "divorce rates among conservative Christians were significantly higher than for other faith groups, and much higher than atheists and agnostics experience." George Barna's statistics were challenged, but he stood by his data, saying, "We rarely find substantial differences" between the moral behavior of Christians and non-Christians (www.religioustolerance.org/chr_dira.htm). A study published by an affiliate of Planned Parenthood says almost a quarter-million abortions are performed each year in the United States on women who identify themselves as born-again or evangelical Christians. According to a startling and little publicized survey by the Alan Guttmacher Institute, 37.4 percent of the abortions are performed on Protestant women, approximately one-half (about 18 percent) of whom profess to be born-again believers. That number accounts for 246,000 aborted babies each year in America (www.edwardbabinski.usarticles/divorce_abortion.html).

20. Wilcox, "The Facts of Life," n.p. Wilcox is assistant professor of sociology at the University of Virginia and is a fellow at the Institute for the Studies of Religion at Baylor University. He is the author of *Soft Patriarchs, New Men*, and has authored numerous articles on religion and family life.

21. Chuck Colson, *How Now Shall We Live* (Wheaton, IL: Tyndale House, 1999), 324. From *The Family in America*, available from the Howard Center for the Family, Religion, and Society, 934 North Main Street, Rockford, IL 61103, phone: (815) 964-5819.

22. For an interesting discussion of rights and the conception of right, see Richard John Neuhaus, "Crisis of the House Divided," *First Things*, no. 106 (October 2000): 84–85.

23. Manfred Marquardt, *John Wesley's Social Ethics: Praxis and Principles* (Nashville: Abingdon Press, 1992), 46.

24. Ibid., 46.

25. Philip E. Johnson, *Reason in the Balance* (Downers Grove, IL: InterVarsity Press, 1995), 149–50.

26. H. T. Maclin, *The World Is Our Parish* (unpublished essay, 2007), 1.

Chapter 7

1. Kenneth Cain Kinghorn, *John Wesley on The Sermon on the Mount: The Standard Sermons in Modern English* (Nashville: Abingdon Press, 2002), vol. 2, 21–33, Discourse 13, "Upon Our Lord's Sermon on the Mount," 293.

2. Ibid.

3. http://www.teenchallengeusa.com.

4. Agnieszka Tennant, "Social Justice Surprise," *Christianity Today* (June 22, 2006): http://www.christianitytoday .com/ct/2006/007/9.44.html.

5. Tim Stafford, "Grandpa John," *Christianity Today* (March 2007): 49–51.

6. Arthur C. Brooks, *Who Really Cares* (New York: Basic Books/Perseus Books Group, 2006), 11, 20–22, 38, 40, 55, 57.

7. Ibid., 12–13.

8. There are two times when Wesley makes reference to "therapeutic." In both instances, Wesley transliterates it from the Greek—*therapeia psuches*—which means "therapy of the soul." "We may learn from hence, in the Third place, what is the proper nature of religion, of the religion of Jesus Christ. It is *therapeia psuches*, God's method of healing a soul which is thus diseased. Hereby the great Physician of souls applies medicines to heal this sickness; to restore human nature, totally corrupted in all its faculties" (from sermon "On Original Sin" VI:64). ". . . and the Christian Revelation speaks of nothing else but the great 'Physician' of our soul; nor can Christian Philosophy, whatever be thought of the Pagan, be more properly defined that in Plato's word: It is *therapeia psuches*, the only true method of healing a distempered soul" (from Preface to The Doctrine Original Sin, IX:194). Both references are from the Jackson edition of Wesley's works.

9. Jean Healan, "Building a National Church in Paraguay," *Good News Magazine*, (May/June 1998): 23–26.

10. New York Plainview UMC has a membership of around 600-650 and an average attendance of 450-500. Camp Paraguay is only one of many outreach programs of this vibrant Korean congregation. The church has three services each Sunday; Wednesday evening service; Friday evening Praise Night; prayer Monday–Saturday at 5:45 AM; Vision College (Bible school for all ages); and Plainview Open Culture Center, which includes classes in Spanish, Chinese Arts, Voice Class, Flower Arrangement, and Finance, among others. The church motto is "seven days-a-week-open church to serve the community." Mission programs include Camp Paraguay; Jesus Village in China (the church bought a small village to create a place for approximately eighty Chinese Christians to live and work in

community); and training for more than one hundred Chinese Christians, thirteen of whom have been selected and commissioned as missionaries to Pakistan and Afghanistan. The church also has other domestic missions in the United States, including a new church plant in New York to reach the next generation.

11. John Wesley, "Of the Church," *The Works of John Wesley*, ed. Thomas Jackson, (London: Wesleyan Methodist Book Room, 1872; reprinted by Baker House, 1978), VI:400–401.

12. Kathleen K. Ruledge, "The Man Behind the Dream," *Good News Magazine* (May/June 2001): 14–20.

13. Charles W. Keysor, "Reaching Those the Church Often Forgets," *Good News Magazine* (September/October 2002): 12–13.

14. Ibid.

15. John Gordon, "Laundromat Ministry Reaches Children and Homeless," *United Methodist News Service* (May 20, 2004): n.p.

Chapter 8

1. Letters, I.284–7 in Henry Carter, *The Methodist Heritage* (Nashville: Abingdon Press, 1951), 139.

2. Letters, I.284–7 in Carter, *The Methodist Heritage*, 139.

3. Journal, VII.59, in Carter, *The Methodist Heritage*, 138.

4. Carter, *The Methodist Heritage*, 55.

5. Ibid., 145.

6. Ibid., 142–143.

7. H. T. Maclin, *The Faith That Compels Us* (Norcross, GA: The Mission Society for United Methodists, 1997), 12.

8. A. H. Oussoren, *William Carey, Especially His Missionary Principles* (Leiden, Neth: A. W. Sijthoff, 1945).

9. William Carey, *An Enquiry into the Obligations of Christians* (London: Hodder and Stoughton, 1891).

10. William L. Woodall, *William Carey of India* (New York: Pageant Press, 1951).

11. J. H. Morrison, *William Carey, Cobbler and Pioneer* (London: Hodder and Stoughton, 1924).

12. J. B. Middlebrook, *William Carey* (London: Carey Kingsgate Press, 1961).

13. Maclin, *The Faith That Compels Us*, 11.

14. Ibid., 12.

15. Church Missionary Society, *A Brief History of the Church Missionary Society* (London: CMS, 1899).

16. Maclin, *The Faith That Compels Us*, 15.

17. Roger S. Guptill, *Though Thousands Fall* (New York: General Conference of the Methodist Episcopal Church, 1928) in Maclin, *The Faith That Compels Us*, 15.

18. Wade C. Barclay, *Early American Methodism, 1769–1844* (New York: Board of Missions and Church Extension of The Methodist Church, 1957).

19. Maclin, *The Faith That Compels Us*, 16.

20. Ibid., 20.

21. For other examples of former staff persons who questioned the political

activism and lack of evangelism of our boards and agencies, see Riley B. Case, *Evangelical and Methodist* (Nashville: Abingdon Press, 2004), chapters 5 and 6.

22. Dean S. Gilliland, ed., *The World Forever Our Parish* (Lexington, KY: Bristol Books, 1991). This quote comes from Gerald H. Anderson, "Toward A.D. 2000 in Mission," 130.

23. www.new.gbgm-umc.org.

24. Mission Personnel Statistics, prepared for the board of directors, April 23–26, 2007, http://new.gbgm-umc.org/about/us/mp/missionaries/statistics.

25. Gilliland, *The World Forever Our Parish*. This quote comes from Gerald H. Anderson, "Toward A.D. 2000 in Mission," 28.

26. International Bulletin of Missionary Research, vol. 31, no. 1, Global Table 5. Status of global mission, presence and activities, AD 1800–2025.

27. Maclin, *The Faith That Compels Us*, 29.

28. Philip Jenkins, "Believing in the Global South," *First Things* (December 2006): no. 168, 13. Jenkins is Distinguished Professor of History at Pennsylvania State University and author of *Decade of Nightmares: The End of the Sixties and the Making of Eighties America*. The quotes and material for this section were adapted from the 2006 Erasmus Lecture, sponsored by First Things and the Institute on Religion and Public Life.

29. Ibid., 16.

30. Ibid.

31. Ibid., 17.

32. Ibid., 14.

33. "Ugandan Diocese Rejects U.S. Funds," *Church Times* (April 2005): Issue 7412. www.churchtimes.co.uk/section.asp?id=4104.

34. "What Is Anglicanism?" Archbishop Henry Luke Orombi, *First Things* (August/September 2007): no. 175, 24.

35. Press Release, "Election of Nigerian United Methodist Bishop Comes Amid Explosive Growth," www.ird-renew.org.

36. Ibid.

Chapter 9

1. Kenneth Cain Kinghorn, "Salvation by Faith," in *John Wesley on Christian Beliefs: The Standard Sermons in Modern English*, vol. 1, 1–20, (Nashville: Abingdon Press, 2002), 44.

2. Ibid., "The Almost Christian," 55.

3. *The Book of Discipline of The United Methodist Church*, 121, 87.

4. Charles Colson and Nancy Pearcey, *How Now Shall We Live?* (Wheaton, IL: Tyndale House Publishers, 1999), 14–15.

5. Ibid., 15.

6. John Wesley, "Of the Gradual Improvement of Natural Philosophy," in *The Works of John Wesley*, ed. Thomas Jackson, 13:487, in Kenneth Cain Kinghorn, *John Wesley on The Sermon on the Mount*, (Nashville: Abingdon Press, 2002), 12.

7. Ibid., 10.

8. Colson and Pearcey, *How Now Shall We Live?*, 17.

9. Steve Harper, *John Wesley's Message for Today* (Grand Rapids: Zondervan

Publishing House, 1983), 139, citing cf. chap. 7, Henry Bett, *The Spirit of Methodism* (London: Epworth Press, 1937).

10. James V. Heidinger II, *United Methodist Renewal: What Will It Take?* (Wilmore, KY: Bristol Books, 1988), 68–69.

11. Kinghorn, "Justification by Faith," 105.

12. Leicester Longden, Assoc. Professor of Evangelism and Discipleship, University of Dubuque Theological Seminary, *The Recovery, Reform, and Renewal of Membership Practices*. This paper was prepared for a Theological Consultation on Membership, Ecclesiology, and Leadership convened by the General Board of Higher Education and Ministry on February 15–16, 2007.

13. Gary A. Haugen, *Good News About Injustice* (Downers Grove, IL: InterVarsity Press, 1999), 35, 48.

14. Ibid., 63.

15. Carl F. H. Henry, "A Summons to Justice," *Christianity Today* (July 20, 1992): 40, in Haugen, *Good News About Injustice*, 64.

16. Dietrich Bonhoeffer, "Ethics," in *First Things* (December 2006): no. 168, 61.

Chapter 10

1. Kenneth Cain Kinghorn, "The Way to the Kingdom," *John Wesley on Christian Beliefs: The Standard Sermons in Modern English* (Nashville: Abingdon Press, 2002), 125.

2. Ibid., 129.

3. Steve Harper, *John Wesley's Message for Today* (Grand Rapids: Zondervan, 1983), 131–138.

4. Ibid., 79.

5. Kinghorn, *John Wesley on Christian Beliefs*, 23.

6. Harper, *John Wesley's Message for Today*, 79.

7. Ibid., 80, citing Telford, *Letters*, 4:90.

8. Thomas Jackson, "The Wilderness State," *The Works of John Wesley* (Grand Rapids: Baker, 1979), 6:81.

9. Harper, *John Wesley's Message for Today*, 80.

10. The Explanatory Notes Upon the New Testament were published in 1755, and the Explanatory Notes Upon the Old Testament followed in 1765.

11. Harper, *John Wesley's Message for Today*, 81.

12. Gary Haugen, *Good News About Injustice* (Downers Grove, Il: InterVarsity Press, 1999), 83.

13. "Americans Draw Theological Beliefs from Diverse Points of View," Barna.org, October 8, 2002, 4.

14. Ibid., 4.

15. "The Bible Literacy Project: What Do Teens Need to Know and What Do They Know?," Bible Literacy Project, 2005, www.Bibleliteracy.org, 7. This study included teachers and students from a geographically broad section of the United States. Racial and religious diversity was represented.

16. Ibid., 8.

17. Ibid., 25.

18. David Gelernter, "Bible Illiteracy in America," *The Weekly Standard* (May 23, 2005): vol. 10, Issue 34, 29. Gelernter is a senior fellow in Jewish thought at the Shalom Center Jerusalem.

19. Harper, *John Wesley's Message for Today*, 82.

20. Ibid.

21. Ibid., 83.

22. Jackson, *The Works of John Wesley*, 3:144.

23. Ibid., 11:433.

24. James V. Heidinger II, *United Methodist Renewal: What Will It Take?* (Wilmore, KY: Bristol Books, 1988) 92, 95.

25. H. T. Maclin, "The World Is Our Parish," (unpublished essay, 2007), 7.

26. Christopher T. Bounds, "The New Testament and the Priority of the Gospel Proclamation," (unpublished essay, 2007), 6–7.

27. H. O. "Tom" Thomas Jr., "The Historical Wesleyan Witness," (unpublished essay, 2007), 12.

28. William R. Cannon, "John Wesley's Message For His Church Today," Gilliland 48, in Maclin, *The Faith That Compels Us*, 106.

Appendix B

1. John Wesley, *the Oxford Edition of the Works of John Wesley*, ed. Frank Baker, vol. 11. *The Appeals to Men of Reason and Religion and Certain Related Open Letters* (Oxford: Clarendon Press, 1975), 46.

2. John Wesley, *The Bicentennial Edition of the Works of John Wesley*, ed. Frank Baker, 34 vols. (Nashville: Abingdon Press, 1984), 2, 493.

3. Wesley, *Appeals*, 128; Wesley, *The Bicentennial Works*, 2, 184.

4. John Wesley, *The Letters of the Reverend John Wesley*, A. M., ed. John Telford, 8 vols. (London: Epworth Press, 1960), 4, 303; see also Wesley, *Letters*, 4, 146; Wesley, *The Bicentennial Works*, 2, 157; 3, 204.

5. Wesley, *The Bicentennial Works*, 2:157. One hastens to say these are not the only doctrines forming the structure of the Gospel message. Nevertheless, the point for our study is that other essential subsidiary doctrines can be generally considered under one or the other of these "two general parts, justification and santification."

6. Randy L. Maddox, *Responsible Grace: John Wesley's Practical Theology* (Nashville: Kingswood Press, 1994), 20f.

7. Thomas Jackson, ed., *The Works of John Wesley*, 3rd ed. (Grand Rapids: Baker Book House, 1979), 7:317; Howe O. Thomas, "John Wesley's and Rudolf Bultmann's Understanding of Justification by Faith Compared and Contrasted" (PhD dissertation, University of Bristol, 1990), 356.

8. Wesley, *The Bicentennial Works*, 1:24.

9. Wesley, *Letters*, 2:186; 3:229; 5:90.

10. Wesley, *Letters*, 4:17.

11. Wesley, *Appeals*, 70.

12. Wesley, *The Bicentennial Works*, 2:158.

13. Ibid., 2, 160–66; *John Wesley, A Plain Account of Christian Perfection*

(Kansas City, MO: Beacon Hill Press, 1966), 55.

14. Wesley, *Letters*, 5:83; Wesley, *Appeals*, 68, 177.

15. Wesley, *The Bicentennial Works*, 3:507.

16. Ibid., 505f.

17. Ibid., 2:38–40.

18. Ibid., 3:393.

19. Manfred Marquardt, *John Wesley's Social Ethics: Praxis and Principles*, trans. John E. Steely and W. Stephen Gunter (Nashville: Abingdon Press, 1992), 119, 136. Marquardt concludes that one of the two aims of Wesley's preaching was "to lead individuals to renewal through God's grace in justification and sanctification . . ."

20. Wesley, *Appeals*, 46; Wesley, *The Bicentennial Works*: 3:295.

21. Ibid., *Appeals*, 45.

22. *The Book of Discipline of the United Methodist Church 2004* (Nashville: The United Methodist Publishing House, 2004), 49.

23. *The Compact Oxford English Dictionary*, second edition.

24. John Wesley, *The Journal of the Rev. John Wesley, A. M.*, standard edition, ed. Nehemiah Curnock (London: The Epworth Press, 1938), 1:151, 475f.

25. Thomas, "Wesley and Bultmann," 421ff.

26. Wesley, *The Bicentennial Works*, 2:385.

27. Ibid., 198f.

28. Ibid., 541f.

29. This has been well recognized by scholars. See Albert C. Outler, ed., *John Wesley* (New York: Oxford University Press, 1964), 209, 29; Kenneth J. Collins, *The Scripture Way of Salvation: The Heart of John Wesley's Theology* (Nashville: Abingdon Press, 1997), 125.

30. Wesley, *The Bicentennial Works*, 1:698.

31. Ibid., 2:168.

32. Thomas, "Wesley and Bultmann," 424.

33. Wesley, *Works*, Jackson, 14, 321.

34. Ibid., 320.

35. Ibid., 320f.

36. Collins, *The Scripture Way*, 159.

37. *The Compact Oxford English Dictionary*, second edition, s. v. "social."

38. Wesley, *Works*, Jackson, 14, 321.

39. Ibid., p. 321.

40. Wesley, *The Bicentennial Works*, 3:295, 291.

41. Ibid., 3:315; Wesley, *Appeals*, 45.

42. Ibid., 46.

43. Wesley, *Works*, 14:541f.

44. Wesley, *The Bicentennial Works*, 1:125; Wesley, *Letters*, 2:227.

45. Wesley, *The Bicentennial Works*, 2, 164; Thomas, "Wesley and Bultmann," 143ff; Collins, *The Scripture Way*, 162; Harald Lindstrom, *Wesley and Sanctification* (Stockholm: Nya Bokforlags Aktiebolaget, 1946), 206.

46. Wesley, *The Bicentennial Works*, 2:164.

47. Wesley, *Letters*, 4:175.

48. Wesley, *The Bicentennial Works*, 3:191; Collins, *The Scripture Way*, 163. Collins's comment that Wesley said works of mercy are to be preferred over works of piety needs clarification.

Wesley did not mean they are in general more desirable or more pleasing to God than works of piety. As the context shows, Wesley was concerned about a temporary conflict between, for example, prayer, and "charity's almighty call." In such a case, one would forgo prayer to "relieve the distress of our neighbour." Wesley goes on to say one should be more zealous for "holy tempers," than "good works." Wesley, *The Bicentennial Works*, 3:314f.

49. Wesley, *The Bicentennial Works*, 1:592f.

50. Ibid., 2, 194f.

51. Ibid., 185; 194f.

52. Ibid., 1:219f.

53. *The Westminster Dictionary of Christian Theology*, 1983 ed., s. v. "Social Gospel."

54. Jose Miguez Bonino, *Doing Theology in a Revolutionary Situation* (Philadelphia: Fortress Press, 1975), 65f, 73, 81. For instance, Bonino suggests the central tenets of the Gospel like "God is Father" and "Jesus died and rose" are addressed not to individual persons but to the collective, to society. The Gospel message is a message to the collective society, not to the individual, as in John Wesley.

55. Wesley, *Works*, 11:154f. Based on Wesley's tract on "Preaching Politics," it is highly doubtful he would approve of the common practice today of denouncing the president, political figures, or their political policies from the pulpit.

56. Roy Porter, *English Society in the Eighteenth Century*, rev. ed. (London: Penguin Books, 1990), 15.

57. Ibid., 86.

58. Ibid., 87; John Wesley, *The Journal of the Rev. John Wesley, A. M.* ed. Nehemiah Curnock (London: The Epworth Press, 1938), 4, 52.

59. Wesley, *The Bicentennial Works*, 3:255.

60. Wesley, *Works*, 8:269.

61. Wesley, *The Bicentennial Works*, 3:254.

62. Wesley, *Journal*, 7:129.

63. Henry D. Rack, *Reasonable Enthusiast: John Wesley and the Rise of Methodism* (Philadelphia: Trinity Press International, 1989), 363.

64. Ibid., 364.

65. Porter, *English Society*, 138f.

66. Wesley, *Journal*, 1:442.

67. Ibid., 4:52.

68. Ibid., 4:355f.

69. Ibid., 3:381ff.

70. Ibid., 3:381–82.

71. Wesley, *The Bicentennial Works*, 3:349.

72. Thomas W. Blanshard, *The Life of Samuel Bradburn, The Methodist Demosthenes* (London: Elliot Stock, 1871), 35. When Samuel Bradburn, a shoemaker and later one of Wesley's helping preachers, began assisting in Methodist preaching, he said he endeavored "to improve myself in the knowledge of the Holy Scriptures, by reading, meditation, and prayer."

73. Porter, *English Society,* 167.

74. Rack, *Reasonable Enthusiast,* 355f, 448; Porter, *English Society,* 166. Also, devoted Methodist Mary Bosanquet supervised a charity school cum orphanage for laborers' children.

75. Abel Stevens, *History of the Methodist Episcopal Church in the United States of America,* 4 vols. (New York: Carlton and Porter, 1864), 2:173.

76. John Abernathy Smith, "Ebenezer Academy: A Methodist School for Virginia," *Virginia United Methodist Heritage,* (2004) XXX, 6ff.

77. Ibid., 11.

78. Wesley, *Works,* 11:59–79.

79. Wesley, *Journal,* 1:244.

80. Wesley, *Journal,* 1:415.

81. Wesley, *Works,* 11:78.

82. Wesley, *Journal,* 7:359f.

83. Wesley, *Letters,* 8:265.

84. Stevens, *History,* 2:77f; 113.

85. Ibid., 2:133.

86. Ibid., 2:249.

87. Ibid., 2:251.

88. Ibid., 2:252; Frederick A. Norwood, *The Story of American Methodism: A History of the United Methodists and Their Relations* (Nashville: Abingdon Press, 1978), 186f.

Appendix C

1. For numerous examples, see Jaroslav Pelikan and Valerie Hotchkiss, eds., *Creeds and Confessions of Faith in the Christian Tradition* (London: Yale University Press, 2003), vol. 2, *Creeds and Confessions of the Reformation Era.*

2. For an excellent discussion of these Roman Catholic and Eastern Orthodox distinctives, see Miroslav Volf, *After Our Likeness: The Church as Image of the Trinity* (Grand Rapids: William B. Eerdmans, 1998), 29–39, 97–126.

3. *The Book of Discipline of The United Methodist Church 2004* (Nashville: The Publishing House of The United Methodist Church, 2004), 62, 67.

4. Unless otherwise specified, all New Testament quotations are taken from Today's New International Version of the Holy Bible (Zondervan and the International Bible Society, 2005).

5. For our discussion of the implicit authority of Jesus and relationship between Jesus and the Kingdom, we are indebted to Gerald O'Collins, *Christology: A Biblical, Historical, and Systematic Study of Jesus* (Oxford: Oxford University Press, 1995), 54–62.

6. For a similar discussion with different nuances on the purpose and role of proclamation in the ministry of Jesus and the New Testament Church, see the Gerhard Friedrich article on preaching in *Theological Dictionary of the New Testament Vol. III,* ed. Gerhard Kittle, trans. Geoffrey Bromiley (Grand Rapids: William B. Eerdmans, 1966), 697–714.

Short Annotated Bibliography

Collins, Kenneth J. *John Wesley: A Theological Journey*. Nashville: Abingdon Press, 2003.

Collins, professor of Wesley Studies and Historical Theology at Asbury Theological Seminary, presents Wesley's theology not topically or in systematic outline, but in historical presentation. Collins examines the development of Wesley's theology across the span of his long and eventful theological career. Clear and well organized, this work examines the primary sources and reflects an intimate knowledge of the different social locations in which Wesley's theological thinking took place.

Harper, Steve. *The Way to Heaven: The Gospel According to John Wesley*. Zondervan, reprinted 2003. Previously published as *John Wesley's Message for Today*.

This book is a thoughtful and inspiring look at Wesley's theology of grace and its power to transform. Included in this updated copy are two new chapters. "Vision and Means," explores Wesley's mission and methods, and "To Serve the Present Age" considers the impact and relevance of his message today. An updated reading list facilitates further study, and questions at the end of each chapter stimulate personal reflection and small group discussion. Ideal as a textbook or for personal study and reflection, this book will advance your knowledge and piety as you travel "the way to heaven."

Kinghorn, Kenneth Cain. *John Wesley on Christian Beliefs*, 3 vol. Nashville: Abingdon Press, 2002.

These three volumes: *John Wesley on Christian Beliefs*, *John Wesley on The Sermon on the Mount*, and *John Wesley on Christian Practice*, make John Wesley's standard sermons accessible to twenty-first century readers. Kinghorn masterfully retains Wesley's original meaning while featuring revised sentence structure, rephrasing of awkward or outdated construction, updated spellings, and "translation" of words whose meanings have changed. In addition, each sermon is preceded by an introduction stating the purpose, location, circumstances, and thrust of the material to follow.

Contributors

Judi Arnold is a laywoman from Guntersville, Alabama. She and her husband, Mike, have been married for thirty-nine years and have two children, Matt and Mollie; and five grandchildren. Judi taught school and worked as a high school guidance counselor for thirty years before retiring. She accepted Christ and was baptized at age twelve in the Christian and Missionary Alliance Church. Judi attended Shades Mountain Independent Church (Methodist) from 1968 until 2000. She and Mike joined Guntersville First UMC in July of 2000. Judi is an active laywoman and has served in church ministry in numerous capacities with all age levels for many years.

Christopher T. Bounds received his PhD from Drew University. He is Associate Professor of Theology at Indiana Wesleyan University in Marion, Indiana. Bounds is an ordained Elder in The Arkansas Conference of The United Methodist Church, where he served as an associate and senior minister for eight years.

H. T. Maclin, and his wife, Alice, were accepted for mission service in 1952. During their nearly twenty-year tenure in Africa, they saw forty-two nations achieve political independence from European powers. After returning to the United States, Maclin was nominated by the General Board of Global Ministries as the Field Representative for Mission Development in the Southeastern Jurisdiction in 1974.

Maclin became the founding president of The Mission Society for United Methodists (now called The Mission Society) in 1984 and served as the chief executive officer until his official retirement in

1991. The Maclins have continued to work as volunteers in such places as Kazakhstan, China, India, Latin America, and other parts of the world.

James R. Thobaben is professor of Church in Society at Asbury Theological Seminary, Wilmore, Kentucky. His expertise is in bioethics, social ethics, sociology of religion and rural life. Thobaben received a BA from Oberlin College; an MDiv from Yale Divinity School, an MPH from Yale Medical School, and a PhD from Emory University. He has pastored in Appalachian Ohio and in rural Kentucky, putting his understanding of social ethics into practice while offering Christ as the foundation of his ministry.

H. O. "Tom" Thomas Jr. has personally known and walked with Jesus for more than thirty-five years. An ordained United Methodist elder, he has pastored seven local church charges in southern California, England, and Virginia. He is also a faculty member of Southside Virginia Community College, teaching courses in the history of theology and Christianity. He was previously an associate professor for five years at Asbury Theological Seminary in Lexington, Kentucky. He received his PhD degree from Bristol University in Bristol, England, where he studied the theology of John Wesley and lived in John Wesley's Chapel "The New Room." He has been married to his wife, Pamela, for thirty years. They have two children, Karissa, seventeen, and John, ten. His prayer is, "Lord, be merciful to me, a sinner."

Kenny Kang Yi was born in South Korea. He graduated from the Hankook University of Foreign Studies and worked in South America, representing a Korean general trading firm. Kenny immigrated to the United States in 1983. He attended and received his MDiv from Drew Theological Seminary in 1992 and also studied at Oral Roberts University, studying in the DMin program. From 1994–2000, Rev. Kang Yi served as senior pastor at Christ United Methodist Church in Staten Island, New York. He is presently senior pastor at the New York Plainview United Methodist Church in Long Island, New York. The churches he serves are very active in national and international missions.

About the Authors

Faye Short

My roots go deep in Methodism. Four generations of my family are buried in the cemetery at Ebenezer United Methodist Church in rural Chambers County, Alabama. My personal Christian history spills over into Methodist-related offshoots, including my experience of saving faith in an Assemblies of God church as a teen and my years of service alongside my husband, Dennis, that began in the Wesleyan Church. Since 1975, we have given pastoral leadership to United Methodist churches in the North Georgia Annual Conference.

While serving in United Methodist Women leadership capacities, I became aware that the programs and policies of the Women's Division did not square with my Wesleyan theological background. I respectfully voiced a dissenting opinion on theological, political, and social issues, knowing that the views I expressed were representative of many women within my conference.

During this time, my husband and I discovered the Good News movement through the *Good News* magazine. We felt at home with this group of United Methodist laity and clergy who self-identified as a "forum for Scriptural Christianity within The United Methodist Church." When I completed my service as a Conference UMW officer, I was asked to become a member of the Good News Board of Directors.

In 1989, I was asked by the chair of the Good News Women's Taskforce to help plan an event for women at an upcoming Good News summer convocation. The event was a huge success under the leadership of Julia Williams, then vice president and later president, of The Mission Society for United Methodists. Julia allowed the women ten minutes to "gripe" before spending the remainder of the time determining what we could do to help make a difference in the women's ministry of our denomination. Afterward, the women mobbed the group leaders asking how they were to execute the event plans. At a follow-up meeting, the Evangelical Coalition for United Methodist Women (ECUMW) was formed. Julia and I became co-directors. Within two years the ECUMW was renamed The RENEW Network, and I became president.

It has been an incredible privilege to lead this network of evangelical women within The United Methodist Church. The core leadership of RENEW consists of talented, dedicated Christian women from across the nation, whose volunteer services enable RENEW to provide the information and resources network members request. Members number in the thousands and represent United Methodist women who are committed to scriptural Christianity and to the reform and revitalization of the women's ministries of The United Methodist Church.

I have been brought full circle back to my Wesleyan roots through the exploration of our Methodist history and rediscovery of the value of a Wesleyan social witness that includes offering Christ. Offering saving faith in today's culture is as relevant as it was when John Wesley delivered his sermon "Salvation by Faith," and as pertinent as when he gave his charge to Thomas Coke to go to America and "Offer them Christ."

Kathryn Kiser

I was reared in the Methodist Church, and my family has roots in the church running more than three generations deep. As I grew up during the 1960s, I witnessed times of social and political upheaval. These issues touched the church as well, and I can remember from an early age my parents' concern that the church was becoming politically sympathetic to ideologies they found totalitarian, atheistic, and opposed to personal liberty. They feared that the Gospel message—that is, the root cause of conflict and oppression is sin embedded in the human heart—was being marginalized.

My faith was severely challenged during my college years in the late 1960s. As I look back on that time, I have come to understand the church somehow assumed I would "catch" what it meant to be a Christian and embrace what Christ had done for me on the cross. I knew I was a believer, but I could not articulate or defend my faith. I was familiar with a good deal of Christ's teaching, but I was lacking a deep understanding of its theological implications. I set out to address my Biblical and theological ignorance.

It was at a UMC women's meeting during the late 1970s that I again became aware of the controversial political issues within the church. Our pastor shared with us a number of political positions that The United Methodist Church had taken. This was my first introduction to the political lobbying done by church boards and agencies and by the Women's Division of the General Board of Global Ministries. I was challenged at that meeting to understand and defend the gospel from the confines of a political agenda. The concerns I had vaguely been aware of began to take shape.

In the 1980s, I learned of the renewal ministries within The United Methodist Church. There was much talk of the historic Christian faith, orthodoxy, the Wesleyan distinctive, ecumenism, theological pluralism, unity, and the like. I began to ask questions about the nature of renewal, the theological principles on which Methodism is based, and whether these principles are still relevant to contemporary Christianity. I continued the search I had begun as a young adult.

I am a lay woman who, from early memory to today, has seen deep division within this denomination. There are many causes for and facets of this division. Disagreement over how we will envision our social witness is just one area. Like many others, I have become concerned about the witness of The United Methodist Church when it appears in some instances to be no more than a partisan political voice in the culture. I believe that concern is shared by United Methodists on every part of the political spectrum. For centuries, Christians have contemplated the role of the church in society, and the application of the gospel to our public lives in our search for justice. We must be wary of partisan agendas that do little more than co-opt the faithful for political action.

It is my hope that the reader of this book will be challenged to re-examine the social witness of The United Methodist Church. I pray the reader will be inspired to study the history of John Wesley and the early Methodist societies and to think deeply about the priorities and commitments that guided them.